W9-BLO-587

THE
EVOLUTION
OF
CHRISTIANITY

THE EVOLUTION OF

CHRISTIANITY

TWELVE CRISES
THAT SHAPED THE CHURCH

MARSHALL D. JOHNSON

continuum

NEW YORK • LONDON

The Continuum International Publishing Group
15 East 26th Street, New York, NY 10010

The Continuum International Publishing Group Ltd
The Tower Building, 11 York Road, London SE1 7NX

Unless otherwise indicated, biblical quotations are from the New Revised Standard Version Bible, copyright 1989, Division of Christian Education of the National Council of the Churches of Christ in the United States of America. Used by permission. All rights reserved.

Cover and interior design: Corey Kent

Library of Congress Cataloging-in-Publication Data

Johnson, Marshall D.
  The evolution of Christianity: twelve crises that shaped the church / Marshall D. Johnson.
    p. cm.
  Includes bibliographical references (p.) and index.
  ISBN 0-8264-1642-X (hardcover)
  1. Church history. I. Title.
  BR145.3J64 2005
  270—dc22

                          2004027182

Printed in the United States of America
05 06 07 08 09 10   10 9 8 7 6 5 4 3 2 1

TO
NATHAN,
CATHERINE,
AND
JENNIFER

Contents

Chronology

All dates are C.E.*

April, 30	death of Jesus
ca. 32**	Paul's conversion
before 44	the first Gentiles join the followers of Jesus
49	apostolic council in Jerusalem; the Gentile mission is approved
62/63	martyrdom of James, the brother of Jesus
ca. 64–65	Nero's persecution of Christians in Rome, martyrdom of Peter
August, 70	destruction of Jerusalem by the Roman general Titus
ca. 117	martyrdom of Ignatius in Rome
ca. 140	activity of Marcion in Rome
February 23, 155	martyrdom of Polycarp of Smyrna
177	persecution of Christians in Gaul by the emperor Marcus Aurelius

---

* The scholarly convention of using B.C.E., "before the Christian era," and C.E., "Christian era," to designate B.C. and A.D., respectively, is followed in this book.

** Ca. (Latin, *circa*) means "approximately."

ca. 180–200	widespread Christian agreement on New Testament canon, creed, and authority of bishops
249–251	first empire-wide Roman persecution of Christians
312	Constantine gains control of the Roman Empire, begins the Christianizing of the empire
325	Council of Nicea
ca. 330	Constantine moves imperial capital to Byzantium, renames it Constantinople; beginning of the Eastern (Byzantine) Empire
Easter, 387	baptism of Augustine
410	fall of Rome to Alaric, Visigoth king and Arian Christian
451	Council of Chalcedon; Roman Pope Leo I
476	the last (Western) Roman emperor deposed by the Ostrogoths
496	conversion of Clovis, king of the Franks
529	Benedict of Nursia (480–543) founds the cloister of Monte Cassino in Italy
590–604	papacy of Gregory the Great
June 622	the Hegira: Muhammad's flight from Mecca to Medina, the beginning of Islam
732	Charles Martel defeats Muslims in the Battle of Tours, France
Christmas, 800	Charlemagne crowned emperor by Pope Leo III
1054	the Great Schism between the Eastern (Orthodox) and Western (Latin, Roman Catholic) churches
1099	capture of Jerusalem in the First Crusade
1198–1216	papacy of Innocent III; strongest claims of papal authority
ca. 1280	end of the Crusades
1309–1377	the Avignon (France) papacy
July 6, 1415	martyrdom of John Huss at the Council of Constance

October 31, 1517 Martin Luther posts his Ninety-five Theses; beginning of the Reformation

1530s   Henry VIII separates the Church of England from Rome

September, 1540 Society of Jesus (Jesuits) is approved by the pope

1541–1564   work of John Calvin at Geneva

1543   death of Nicolaus Copernicus and publication of his theory of heliocentricity

1545–1563   Council of Trent, part of the Counter-Reformation

1555   the Peace of Augsburg recognizes Lutheranism and Catholicism in Germany

1648   the Peace of Westphalia ends the Thirty Years War and recognizes Calvinists along with Lutherans and Catholics

1789   the Constitution of the United States provides for religious freedom and the disestablishment of religion

1856–1939   Sigmund Freud

1859   Charles Darwin (1809–1882) publishes *The Origin of the Species*

1948   the World Council of Churches is founded in Amsterdam

Preface

Established institutions and ideologies often have evolved out of controversy and conflict, which proves that nothing can solidify a point of view more effectively than a confrontation with its opponents. That this is the case with Western Christian theology is the assumption and organizing principle of this book.

Owing to limitations of space and the intended readership of this book, I have found it necessary to give less than sufficient attention to the great tradition of Eastern Orthodox Christianity, which I think has a most cogent claim to stand in direct historical succession from the apostolic age. I have nonetheless aimed at conveying a general impression of the hallmarks of Orthodox piety as well as the historical significance of the events that culminated in the Great Schism of 1054. Similarly, the rapid growth of Christianity in Africa and in parts of southeast Asia in the past two hundred years has had to be left out of the consideration to which it is due.[1]

Although informed readers might want any number of other topics to be more thoroughly treated, the twelve crises described in this book offer an intelligible picture of how Christian theology, especially in its Western form, got to be what it is today and thereby enable the reader to pursue matters of special interest in greater depth.

Hearty thanks go to Dr. C. Arthur Christiansen for his careful reading of the manuscript. I am indebted also to Henry Carrigan, Amy Wagner, and other members of the expert publishing team at Continuum for their advice, their promptness, and their meticulous attention to detail.

INTRODUCTION
History as a Response to Crises

The term *history* has a variety of meanings. On the absolute level, it means everything that has happened—"absolute history." This is obviously an abstraction. We cannot know everything that has happened because available sources permit a reconstruction of only a minute part of the past.

On the residual level, history refers to the artifacts, such as manuscripts, potsherds, inscriptions, coins, buildings, and ruins, that remain of the past. Residual history is a subset of absolute history.

On the academic level, history is a discipline. Sometimes it is considered a science and sometimes an art.

On the written or oral level, history is the interpretation of a selected part of the past, which can range from the oral traditions of a nomadic tribe to a technical dissertation at an institution of higher learning. The best historical research often involves the shaping of a thesis as the answer to a contemporary question and the gathering of evidence in support of the thesis. History thus understood is a dynamic system of meanings, an analysis of significant events, persons, ideas, or social realities of the past that is intended to provide orientation to our present and guide our conduct into the future.

History is important for self-understanding—to help us see how we have come to the place where we are. We cannot understand what we are until we know what we have been, which is to say that we become human only when we come to terms with our past. Awareness of our past can often similarly help us discern trends that will continue into the future.

The study of history can also help us achieve a realistic humility about our place in the sweep of things. Even if a person should survive for a full century, that lifetime is but the blink of an eye in geological time or world-historical time. Our age is not necessarily "better" than some eras of the past, nor are our ideas and innovations always as new as we might think.

In the final analysis history is best studied as an intellectual adventure. The ability to relive debates of the past, to reconstruct living conditions of an ancient group, or to penetrate the mind of a great thinker is a pleasure in itself. As Simone de Beauvoir has convincingly demonstrated, if you approach old age without interests beyond self, you will not have a fulfilling life, and if you have not developed such interests before the age of thirty, you probably never will.[1]

The study of *Christian* history has its own distinctive functions. It can force the tradition-bound Christian to greater awareness of the complexity of doctrinal issues and of the rather ordinary and sometimes predictable evolution of church structures and beliefs. Knowledge of Christian history also has value for secularized persons of the twenty-first century who are not aware of the debt of Western society to Christian, and Jewish, values. Readers today are often amazed to learn of the varieties of beliefs among early Christian groups, the conflicts that gave rise to early Christian creeds, the development of church hierarchies, and the implications of the alliance of church and state begun by Constantine in the first half of the fourth century. Historical knowledge is essential for meaningful discussion among Christians of various persuasions and also between Christians and secularists.

How—and with what assumptions—should history be studied? Subjective elements cannot be avoided. There are topics to be selected, questions to be framed, sources to be sifted, prejudices to be exposed, and judgments to be made—all of which involve subjectivity. Christians have generally taken one of three basic approaches to the study of their history:

1. Traditionalists have followed the dictum of Vincent of Lérins who, in the middle of the fourth century, offered this principle when arguing that Augustine's theology was dangerous: "The church teaches what has been believed everywhere, always, and by all." For him this was "the norm of ecclesiastical and catholic opinion."[2] Such an approach presupposes that there was no serious difference in doctrine between the apostolic period of New Testament times and the Christian theologians and leaders of later centuries. Doctrine and dogma do not evolve; there always has been an "orthodox" Christianity that has never contradicted itself. The understanding of doctrine might unfold and the latent truth become more explicitly stated, but dogma—truth—is unchangeable.

2. Other Christians have assumed that the teachings of Jesus and the original apostles represent a golden age, the highest norm for Christian faith and life of all ages. According to this view, the purest expression of the gospel, found especially in the writings of Paul and John, was corrupted by later Christian writers by an increasing emphasis on monasticism, hierarchical authority, the merit of good works, and such. In earlier centuries, this view was sometimes supported by the mistaken belief that there was a considerable gap of time between the writing of the New Testament and the next oldest Christian writings.

3. A variant of the second approach was held by liberal schools of thought in the early twentieth century. According to this view, Christianity consists of adherence to the simple, moral teachings of Jesus (rather than, for example, beliefs about his death and resurrection). Jesus, a Jewish reformer, sought to win human beings for God so that they could live for others. This simple gospel, however, was soon beclouded by those who were more interested in dogma than in morality, so that church history is

the story of the "fall" from the teachings *of* Jesus to doctrines *about* him.

The assumption of this book is that there has been a development both of doctrine and of church structures throughout history and

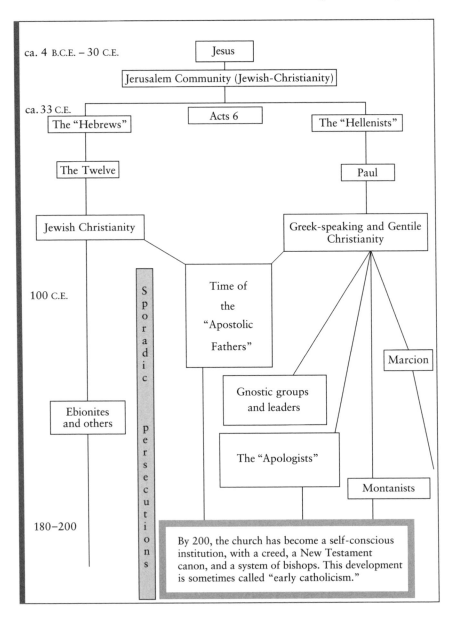

that the main stimulus for change was conflict. Jesus lived and thought in a Jewish milieu, but the church soon became a largely Gentile movement. Christianity took on a distinctive shape in each major locality to which it spread, and the resulting differences often erupted in conflict. This means that the church historian must consider the specific location from which the primary sources come. Doing church history by site—the diachronic method of tracing the historical development of one major church center at a time—is a most appropriate and fruitful approach, although in a book of this scope it is scarcely possible to follow this method consistently.

As the variety of Christian belief became increasingly greater and more complex, pressures grew to develop criteria by which to distinguish tolerable teachings from heresy, criteria that were adopted by Christian churches in several parts of the Mediterranean world between the years 180 and 200. This development can be expressed in the diagram that appears on the previous page.

Behind every formal creed, every advance in the fine-tuning of the hierarchical structure of the church, and every schism, we can expect to find a lively conflict between opposing groups or individuals. And the history of Christian theology—like that of all historical writing—is to a large degree the story of who won.

1

FROM JESUS TO
THE APOSTOLIC FATHERS
The Crisis of Birth and Adolescence

Remember, O Lord, your church:
deliver her from all evil,
perfect her in your love,
and from the four winds gather her, the sanctified, in your kingdom
which you have prepared for her.
For yours is the power and the glory for evermore.

—*Didache* 10:5[1]

The issue: What new thing, if any, would emerge from the activity of Jesus and his earliest followers, and what would be its relation to Judaism?

What we know today as Christianity first emerged as an unnamed new sect from the womb of its mother, Judaism. The belief by Jesus' immediate followers in the exaltation (resurrection) of Jesus after death marks the birth of Christianity, and the period from then, about 30 C.E., to about 180 C.E. functions as its adolescence. As with any newborn, this "Jesus movement" had to find its way in a strange world and cultivate its independence from its parent.

The first tensions within the new community of which we have any information were intramural, between the two groups mentioned in Acts 6, the "Hebrews" and the "Hellenists," both of which were Jewish. When early leaders of the movement made the momentous decision to admit Gentiles who did not follow the Jewish law, conflict heightened, both within the group and in its relations to Jewish communities on the outside. During its first one hundred years the Jesus people evolved from a Jewish sect to a largely Gentile movement with the growing realization that it was becoming a "church," a new religion.

Jesus

Even though he certainly would not have recognized the forms of the movement that had developed in his name within one or two centuries after his death, the fact remains that Jesus stands at the beginning of Christian history.

What can be known about the historical figure of Jesus is one of the most heatedly debated questions of the past several decades. Non-Christian sources provide almost no information that is independent of the Christian Gospels, even though there are several intriguing statements about Jesus by Roman writers and also in the Talmud. With the possible exception of the second-century Gospel of Thomas, the gospels outside of the New Testament shed little light on the Jesus of history. And the interpretation of the New Testament gospels—Matthew, Mark, Luke, and John—is problematic. John is a highly theological writing. The other three, known as the Synoptic Gospels because of their common perspective, were similarly written to convince readers of the truth of Christian claims about Jesus. Moreover, it is almost certain that none of the Gospels was written by an eyewitness of Jesus' ministry (both Matthew and Luke use the Gospel of Mark as a major source, and Mark is nowhere claimed to have been an eyewitness). All four Gospels are anonymous documents, written to serve the needs of an expanding church in the latter half of the first century.

Some aspects of the outward events of Jesus' life are firmly grounded: He was born within a few years of 4 B.C.E. He was a Galilean from Nazareth. On a trip south to Judea he was influenced by John the Baptist and was baptized. After John's arrest Jesus began to preach in Galilee and gathered about himself a small group of loyal disciples. He performed acts of healing and exorcism and preached good news to the downtrodden and hopeless. As Passover in the year 30 C.E. approached, he entered the temple in Jerusalem, protesting the arrangements for sacrifice and antagonizing many in authority. He was executed in Jerusalem, probably on Friday, April 7, in the year 30, by order of the Roman prefect Pontius Pilate (who held office 26–36 C.E.). Within weeks of his death, his earliest followers proclaimed that God had raised him from the dead.

Jesus' preaching and his basic motivation centered on the imminence of the "kingdom" (effective rule) of God in this world (see Mark 1:14–15). Jesus saw the healings he performed as signs of God's overcoming of evil. He told parables to impress on his hearers the crisis that the kingdom would bring and he taught a stringent, humanitarian morality as a means of preparing for life in the kingdom. He spoke of the possibility of immediate access to God as a gracious Father. Some sayings in the Gospels, such as Mark 9:1 and 14:25, suggest that Jesus looked for the end of all forms of evil—the coming of the kingdom of God—in the near future.

Jesus' Resurrection as the Birth of the Christian Church

All early Christians believed that God had exalted Jesus after his death and taken him into his presence, and they struggled to understand and explain this.[2] For the early Christians, two kinds of evidence supported their belief in the resurrection of Jesus: narratives of the discovery of the empty tomb and reports of his appearances to believers.

The discovery of the empty tomb is reported in all four gospels, with curious differences of detail regarding

- the names and number of women who visited the tomb (Mark mentions three by name: two Marys and Salome; Matthew: the two Marys; Luke: at least five; John: Mary Magdalene only [but she uses the pronoun "we" in 20:2]);
- the degree of darkness when the women arrived (Mark: "when the sun had risen"; John: "while it was still dark");
- why the women went to the tomb (Mark and Luke: to anoint the body; Matthew: to see the tomb; John: unspecified);
- the figure or figures the women saw at the tomb (Mark: "a young man"; Matthew: "an angel of the Lord"; Luke: "two men"; John: "two angels");
- the conversation between the figure(s) and the women;
- and what the women then did (Mark: "they said nothing to anyone, for they were afraid"; Matthew: "they left the tomb quickly with fear and great joy, and ran to tell his disciples"; Luke: "they told all this to the eleven and to all the rest"; John: "Mary Magdalene went and announced to the disciples, 'I have seen the Lord' ").

Various theories have been suggested to account for these differences and for the origin of the empty tomb tradition as a whole. Suggestions that the women visited the wrong tomb ("He is not here"), that Jesus had not really died but had awakened and left, or that the disciples invented the story as a fraud are not convincing. Although each gospel writer draws on traditions distinctive to a specific locale, Mark's narrative appears to be the basis of each of the others. It is striking that Mary Magdalene is the common factor in all versions of the story. In any case, all four accounts of the discovery of the empty tomb reflect the genuine and universal conviction of all of the earliest Christians that God had raised Jesus from the dead and brought him to the presence of God.

The Christian belief in the exaltation of Jesus by God, however, is not identical with belief in the empty tomb, which leads merely to the conviction that the body of Jesus was not there. How the early Christians understood the fate of Jesus is seen most clearly in accounts of the appearances of the risen Jesus to his followers.

Appearances of the risen Christ are referred to in Matthew, Luke, John, Acts, and the letters of Paul. If, as seems likely, Mark's Gospel originally ended at 16:8, it had no narratives of resurrection appearances, but Mark twice (14:28; 16:7) anticipates such an appearance to Peter in Galilee.

Luke names Cleopas and his companion as the first to see the risen Christ (Luke 24:13–35), while in John it is Mary Magdalene (John 20:14). There are differing conceptions also of the risen body: Although in Luke and John, Jesus appears and disappears at will (Luke 24:13–53; John 20:19), Luke also reports that the risen Jesus ate broiled fish (Luke 24:43) and had "flesh and bones" (Luke 24:39), and John has doubting Thomas feel the wounds in his body. Paul, however, insists that "flesh and blood cannot inherit the kingdom of God" (1 Cor 15:50), that what is involved is a "spiritual body" (1 Cor 15:44), and that Christ will change the bodies of the believers to be like his glorified body (1 Cor 15:49–55).

The oldest and most detailed list of witnesses of such appearances, however, is Paul's in 1 Cor 15:3–11. Paul apparently intended the items in his list to be read as occurring in sequence:

- Cephas (the Aramaic name for the Greek translation "Peter"; both mean "rock"),
- the Twelve,
- more than five hundred persons at one time, "most of whom are still alive,"
- James (Jesus' brother, not one of the Twelve),
- "all the apostles,"
- and Paul.

This list, which Paul says was transmitted to him, possibly at the time he joined the church, might be composed of two originally separate lists of three items each. There is a balance between Peter and James, "the Twelve" and "all the apostles," and somewhat irregular appearances to others. That Peter was the first witness of the resurrected Jesus is suggested also by Mark 14:28 and 16:7, and appearances to the eleven disciples are reported also in Matthew, Luke, and

John. Paul, whose letters are the earliest documents of the Christian community, interprets his conversion as an appearance of the risen Jesus. Paul insists, moreover, that the kind of "spiritual body" (1 Cor 15:44) all believers would be granted in their resurrection would be the same as the glorified body of the risen Jesus.

The Jerusalem Church and Jewish Christianity

The New Testament book of Acts is the only source available for our knowledge of the earliest Christian community, the church of Jerusalem. The material in Acts is divided between the earliest Jerusalem church—symbolized by the figure of Peter (roughly, Acts 1–15)—and the missionary work of Paul among Gentiles and hellenized Jews throughout Asia Minor and Greece (roughly, Acts 9–28).

According to Acts, the church in Jerusalem began its missionary activity at the Jewish festival of Pentecost, about seven weeks after Passover—in this case seven weeks after the crucifixion. At that time, a large number of Jewish pilgrims from various parts of the world joined the nascent group of believers. They continued to participate with other Jews in temple worship (Acts 2:46; 3:1–10; 4:1; 5:20–21, 42) but met separately as believers in Jesus for a common meal and fellowship (Acts 2:42, 46). Peter, to whom the author attributes a powerful sermon on the day of Pentecost, was the dominant figure in the Jerusalem church from the beginning.

A slight crack in the picture of an idealized unity among the first believers emerges for the first time in Acts 6, which describes a dispute between the "Hellenists" (presumably Greek-speaking Jews from outside Palestine) and the "Hebrews" (Palestinian, Aramaic-speaking Jews). Jewish leaders accused Stephen, the presumed leader of the Hellenists, of speaking against the temple and the law of Moses (6:13), an accusation prompted, possibly, by what may have been the Hellenists' less ethnic conception of the Jesus movement compared to that of the Hebrews. Stephen was condemned by the "council" (6:12) and, after making the longest speech in the book (Acts 7:2–53), was stoned to death, becoming the first in a long line of Christian martyrs.

The result of Stephen's death was further persecution, which drove some of the apostles out of Jerusalem, resulting in the spread of the church beyond Jerusalem and even into Samaria, home of a people of mixed or questionable Israelite identity.

In 44 C.E. the political leader Herod Antipas, grandson of Herod the Great, led a persecution of believers in which several leaders were executed, including one of the Twelve, James, brother of John. Peter was imprisoned but escaped. At this point, the leadership of the Jerusalem church passed to Jesus' brother James, known to many Jews as James the Just.

By 44 C.E. a major event in Christian history had taken place: the first Gentile had been accepted into the church. This was Cornelius, a Roman soldier who was brought into the church without becoming circumcised (the initiation ceremony for males who become Jews) by Peter at Caesarea, according to the narrative of Acts 10. The Jesus movement was now not purely a Jewish group. Other Gentiles would soon join the church, and Antioch became a center of Gentile Christianity; it was there that the term "Christian" was first used of the believers (Acts 11:26).

Whether non-Jewish persons should be accepted into the church without being circumcised, however, was a hotly debated issue. According to Acts 15, Christian leaders gathered in Jerusalem in about 49 C.E. to settle the matter. After heated discussion, James issued the decree that Gentiles could become Christians without first becoming Jews, but that they should observe the laws that the Torah assigns to Noah, the father of all humanity (Acts 15:28–29; see Gen 9:3–7). Christianity would now inevitably become a largely Gentile movement.

In 62/63 C.E. James, brother of Jesus, was murdered at the instigation of the high priest Ananus.[3] Leadership of the Jerusalem church then appears to have passed to Jesus' cousin Simeon bar Clopas (presumably a son of Joseph's brother), who was accepted as head of the Jewish Christians until his crucifixion by the emperor Trajan's governor, Atticus, in 107 C.E.[4]

A crisis of major proportions for Jews and Christians alike was the Jewish-Roman War of 66–73 C.E. The Roman generals Vespasian and his son Titus—both destined to become emperors—defeated Jewish armies in Galilee and, in August 70 C.E., captured and totally destroyed Jerusalem, including the temple and its system of animal sacrifices. According to the Christian historian Eusebius, Jewish Christians fled Jerusalem before its fall and migrated to Pella, in the Jordan Valley not far from the Sea of Galilee.

The daunting task of reconstructing Judaism without a temple and without a land was undertaken after the war by the Pharisees. One of their actions presumably was to insert into the synagogue service the Birkath ha-Minim, a curse of the "heretics," which Christians were unwilling to recite.

Jewish Christians of the second and later centuries came to be known by other Christians as Ebionites ("the poor") and—ironically—were considered heretics. This group (or groups) emphasized the binding character of the law of Moses, rejected the letters of Paul, accepted only the Gospel of Matthew, strongly repudiated bloody sacrifices (which for them meant rejecting a theology of the cross), and at least some espoused vegetarianism. They believed that Jesus was the human son of Joseph and Mary upon whom the Holy Spirit had descended in a unique way at his baptism. He was the "righteous one," the "servant of God," and appointed to become the Messiah. God raised him from the dead as a reward for his perfect life. The main function of Jesus, according to the Ebionites, was to reform the law of Moses by removing accretions subsequent to Moses and giving the law its true interpretation. Although such Jesus groups were quite different from the Christian communities that developed on Gentile soil, they gave Christianity many of its permanent institutions, including the rites of baptism and the Lord's Supper, other forms of worship, an orientation to history, and the tradition of social welfare.[5]

Paul and the Emergence of Gentile Christianity

The second section of Acts describes the energy of the missionary Paul in increasing the numbers of Gentile converts throughout the eastern part of the Mediterranean world, activity that brought quantum changes to the theology and life of the new faith.[6] The reader of Acts has the rare opportunity of comparing the account in chapters 9–28 with Paul's own letters. Among the details found only in Acts—not mentioned in the letters—are Paul's hometown, Tarsus (Acts 9:11, 30; 11:25; 21:39; 22:3), his Roman citizenship (16:37–38; 22:25–29; 23:27), his study in Jerusalem with the great Jewish teacher Gamaliel (22:3; Paul himself takes pride in his background as a Pharisee; see Phil 3:5–6), his trade, tentmaking (Acts 18:3), and his Hebrew name, Saul (see 13:9). In addition, Paul's speeches in Acts demonstrate a quite different understanding of the new faith compared with his letters. All of these details raise the question of the relation between historical information and literary artifice in the book of Acts. The picture of Paul in Acts, however, is strikingly and artfully done.

Paul's coming to faith in Jesus is narrated three times (Acts 9; 22; 26). It occurred near Damascus, where Paul, as a persecutor of followers of Jesus, was going to seek out believers. According to Acts and Paul's own statements (Gal 1:14–17; 1 Cor 9:1; 15:8), the risen Jesus appeared to him and commissioned him to be "apostle to the Gentiles." This revelation forced Paul to a radical switch of loyalties—from persecution of the Jesus movement out of zeal for the Torah to fierce and untiring evangelism for the gospel.

Acts structures Paul's travels into three missionary journeys and a final journey to Rome. The first journey (Acts 13:1–14:28) took him to Cyprus and then to what is now the south-central part of Turkey. His pattern when reaching a town was to seek out the synagogue and there appeal mainly to the adherents of Gentile background, arguing for the resurrection of Jesus and his messiahship. The second journey (Acts 15:36–18:22) took him through the places of the first journey and then to Europe (Philippi, Athens, and Corinth, in Greece). On the third journey (Acts 18:23–21:17) Paul visited most of the churches he had founded on the first two and—most probably—wrote his greatest surviving letters. He returned by sea from Miletus in Asia Minor to Jerusalem with a collection of money from his Gentile converts to aid the church in Jerusalem, which was suffering from famine and poverty at the time. On his arrival in Jerusalem, Paul was arrested, brought to a Jewish council (22:30), taken to the Roman governor at Caesarea, Felix (23:23–24), and, after two years' delay, brought before Felix's successor, Festus (24:27). On the basis of his Roman citizenship (23:27), Paul insisted that his case be tried in Rome (25:9–12), and Festus concurred. Paul's final journey in Acts (chapter 27) is a vivid account of sea travel in antiquity. Paul arrived in Rome (28:16), was kept under house arrest, yet was free to preach (28:16, 30–31).

By all accounts, Paul was a Hellenistic Jew who became the most influential Christian missionary to the Gentiles. Owing largely to his efforts, Christianity was transformed into a religion that did not require adherence to the law of Moses, but instead emphasized redemption—freedom from sin, death, and the law—wrought by God through the death of Jesus. A mystical element came to characterize many groups of the new religion, with devotion to the exalted Christ at the center.

Varieties of Christology

The variety of beliefs about Jesus among the early Christians can be expressed in diagram form (p. 11).

The Apostolic Fathers

By the end of the first century, Christian communities had emerged throughout the eastern half of the Mediterranean world. The diversity of life and faith among these communities is witnessed by the earliest surviving Christian documents outside of the New Testament. Among the most significant are those that have come to be known as the Apostolic Fathers, so-called since the seventeenth century because the authors were thought to have been disciples of the twelve apostles. As late as the fourth or fifth centuries several of these writings were actually used as Scripture by some Christians.[7]

	Preexistence	Earthly life	Exalted state
Earliest Christianity (fragments of sources in Acts, 1 Peter, and others)	No mention	The predicted servant of God; life ends in the ignominy of the cross	Exalted at the resurrection to the "right hand of God"; awaits return as Messiah
Paul	Was with God from the beginning as divine Wisdom and "Spirit of God"	God's obedient servant; life ends in the ignominy of the cross	Exalted as Son of God at his resurrection; believers are united with Christ
Mark	No mention	Son of God with power from the time of baptism, concealed from humans	Resurrected, but not interpreted
Matthew and Luke	No mention	Humiliation and glory from the time of his virgin birth	Ascended to the right hand of God; awaits return as judge
John	Preexistent *Logos* (Word), agent of creation	Full divine glory perceived by believers	At resurrection, return to "the Father," union with believers

The *Didache*

The only complete manuscript of the ancient and significant document known as the *Didache* was discovered in 1873. The title on the outside of the manuscript scroll is "Teaching [Greek: *didachē*] of the Twelve Apostles," while the fuller title at the start of the text is "Teaching of the Lord [Given] by the Twelve Apostles to the Gentiles." The *Didache* might well be the oldest Christian writing outside of the New Testament, with all or part of its text possibly dating from the first century. Its affinity to the Gospel of Matthew suggests an origin in the area north of Palestine—perhaps Syria.

The *Didache* has three parts:

- Chapters 1–6 consist of ethical teachings for catechumens (persons preparing for baptism). This section is structured on the ancient pattern of the "two ways": "Two ways there are, one of life and one of death, and there is a great difference between the two ways. Now, the way of life is this: first, love the God who made you; secondly, your neighbor as yourself. Do not do to another what you do not wish to be done to yourself" (1:1–2). Jesus' two "great commandments" and the Golden Rule are followed by moral maxims reminiscent of Jesus' teachings in Matthew. Included in this section is the prohibition of abortion ("Do not kill a child by abortion," 2:2; see also *Barn.* 19:5). The section ends with a briefer explanation of "the way of death" (chapter 5) and a conclusion (chapter 6).
- Chapters 7–15 concentrate on guidelines for Christian worship and leaders. That chapters 1–6 were used to instruct candidates for baptism is indicated by 7:1: "Regarding baptism, baptize as follows: *After first explaining all these things,*[8] baptize 'in the name of the Father and of the Son and of the Holy Spirit,' in running water. But if you have no running water, baptize in other water; and if you cannot in cold, then in warm. But if you have neither, pour water over the head three times in the name of the Father and of the Son and of the Holy Spirit" (7:1–3). Chapter 8 commends fasting and praying. It includes the full text of the Lord's Prayer (8:2) and is similar in wording to that of Matt 6:9–13, with the injunction, "Say this prayer three times a day" (8:3). Chapters 9–10 include eloquent prayers to be used in celebrating the "Eucharist" (the Greek term for "thanksgiving," 8:1), the sacred meal, the Lord's Supper. Chapters 11–15 offer practical guidelines for treating visiting teachers (11:1–2) and "apostles and prophets" (11:3–13:7). Whichever itinerant stays more than two days or asks for money is a false prophet. Chapter 14 enjoins worship, including the Eucharist, on "the Lord's Day," that is, Sunday, the day of Jesus' resurrection. Individuals who have a grudge against a co-believer, however, are excluded.

Chapter 15 provides for the appointment of "bishops and deacons worthy of the Lord." These are to be held in honor along with the "prophets and teachers."

- Chapter 16 is a warning to watchfulness in view of the imminent return of the Lord, with its accompanying woes.

1 Clement

The salutation in *1 Clement* indicates that it is an official letter from the Roman church to the church at Corinth. Early Christian tradition attributes the writing to Clement, who, according to early lists of bishops, was bishop of Rome at the end of the first century. Because chapter 44 refers to elders (presbyters) who were appointed by the apostles and still alive at the time of writing, the document is usually dated to roughly 95–100 C.E. The reference to current persecution in 1:1 is sometimes related to actions taken late in his reign by the emperor Domitian (81–96) against Christians in Rome.

The purpose of the long (45 chapters) letter is mainly to deal with a factional crisis, a kind of generation gap, in the Corinthian church. Older bishops had been deposed, and Clement urges the members to reinstate them because they were ordained by God.

The letter is important for its quotations of sayings of Jesus, of Paul's letters, and of the letter to the Hebrews, but especially for the study of the history of the Christian ministry. By the third and fourth centuries, Christians had three major offices of clergy: bishop (Greek: *episkopos*), elder (Greek: *presbyteros*), and deacon (Greek: *diakonos*), of which the bishops, as successors of the apostles, had supreme authority. All three terms occur in *1 Clement*, but no clear distinction can easily be made among them.

The Shepherd of Hermas

Although written in apocalyptic style, with visions, symbols, and homespun allegories, the content of the strange book known as *The Shepherd of Hermas* is almost entirely moralistic. The author, a Roman prophet named Hermas, was, according to late second-century tradition, the brother of Pius, bishop of Rome about 140

C.E. Amazingly to some readers today, the work was accepted as inspired Scripture by many early church leaders and is included among the New Testament writings in the Codex Sinaiticus, a fourth-century manuscript.

The book has three main parts: five visions (allegories of the church and of virtues), twelve commandments, and ten parables (allegories). The whole of the revelation that comes to Hermas is mediated by two figures. In the first four visions, the revealer is a woman named Rhoda, identified by Hermas as his one-time mistress when she had been a slave. She first appears as an elderly woman, but gradually becomes young and beautiful. She represents the church. From the fifth vision to the end, the revealer is clothed as a shepherd and is called the angel of repentance. This figure gives the document its name.

Several striking features of *The Shepherd of Hermas* can be observed:

- Personal virtues, which are represented in *The Shepherd of Hermas* by seven attractive maidens, were already considered important in Christian life. Hermas, however, is the first Christian moralist to foster the idea that good works done beyond what is required (works of supererogation)—for example, not remarrying after the death of one's spouse, or fasting to provide food for the poor and needy—bring additional reward to the individual.

- One of the burning questions of the time, made acute when Christians lapsed under persecution (committed apostasy) or committed murder or adultery, was whether a person who commits a gross sin after baptism could be forgiven. Hermas, in an apparent attempt to find a compromise, taught that this could happen only once.

- Hermas reflects a church that was a less than perfect society. He reprimands the church's hierarchy for greed and political manipulation and comments on his own sins and those of his family.

- Among the distinctive teachings of this book are two that stand out: (1) The apostles after their deaths preached to and baptized those who had died before them (this is a kind of extension of the idea that Christ descended into Hades after his crucifixion); (2) For Hermas, "Christ" and "the Son of God" are one and the same, at least until the incarnation.

Hermas is an invaluable source for our knowledge of the social and religious situation of the Roman church in the middle of the second century, especially the life of average Christians and an average congregation.

Epistle of Barnabas

Wrongly attributed to Paul's traveling companion (see 1 Cor 9:6) in earlier tradition, *Barnabas* is a general treatise that reflects concepts associated with the church at Alexandria ca. 130–140 C.E. Replete with quotations from the Greek Old Testament and symbolic interpretations of such passages, the book concentrates on the relationship between Christianity and Judaism. The author is concerned to show how the law of Moses had been misinterpreted in Judaism. It was never intended to be obeyed literally and was now fulfilled in Jesus. True interpretation involves allegory and symbols so that the text can be shown to refer to Jesus and the church. The relationship with Judaism is completely severed, so that it can be said in this document that God had nothing to do with the founding of Judaism. In spite of its naïve and confused thinking, *Barnabas* was read as authoritative by leaders of the Egyptian church, including Clement of Alexandria and Origen.

Epistle of Polycarp and Martyrdom of Polycarp

Polycarp, bishop of Smyrna in Asia Minor for forty years, was put to death at the age of eighty-six by the Romans on February 23, 155 C.E. According to strong Christian tradition, he was a disciple of the apostle John in Ephesus and a close friend of Ignatius of Antioch.

The *Epistle of Polycarp* to the church in Philippi was written ca. 117. Polycarp inquires about Ignatius, whom Polycarp had met when Ignatius and his captors had stopped in Smyrna on their way to Rome, where Ignatius was later martyred. In particular, Polycarp wants to know whether or not the Philippians have received any letters from Ignatius. Polycarp also urges the Philippian Christians to avoid dissension and cultivate harmony among themselves.

The *Martyrdom of Polycarp* is the earliest known example of what came to be a venerable literary form for the Christians, hagiography (writings about the saints) or acts of martyrs. It is, in good part, an eyewitness account of Polycarp's martyrdom, composed in the name of the church of Smyrna by a certain Marcion, written down by Evarestus, and sent to the Christians at Philomelium in Phrygia.

Compared with later written acts of martyrs, the *Martyrdom of Polycarp* is remarkably free of prodigies and other miraculous details. It is nonetheless permeated with parallels to the sufferings and death of Jesus. Unlike Ignatius, Polycarp attempted to escape martyrdom. And, as Polycarp died, a dove was seen to ascend from his body (chapter 16), a detail that does not in itself argue against eyewitness testimony. The *Martyrdom of Polycarp* is a historical document of the first rank and a gripping witness to the faith of a noble leader in the early church.

Ignatius of Antioch (died ca. 107 C.E.)

Ignatius wrote seven letters while traveling through Asia Minor as he was being taken from Antioch in Syria to Rome to fight and die in the wild-beast shows. Church historian Eusebius of Caesarea reports that Ignatius died during the reign of Trajan (98–117 C.E.) and that he was the second bishop of Antioch after Peter (Origen of Alexandria says that Ignatius was Peter's immediate successor there).

The seven letters—addressed to Ephesus, Magnesia, Tralles, Rome, Philadelphia, Smyrna, and Philippi—are among the best known of early Christian literature. All are written in acute anticipation of his martyrdom. Ignatius urges the Romans to refrain from any attempts to save him from martyrdom. The other letters are written mainly to thank the recipients for their kindness to him on his journey.

The letters are intense, sensitive, mystical, personal, and overflowing with reflective spirituality. They exhibit an overt martyr complex: "Allow me to be eaten by beasts, through whom I can attain to God. I am God's wheat, and I am ground by the teeth of wild beasts that I may be found pure bread of Christ. Rather entice the wild beasts that they may become my tomb and leave no trace of my body, that when I fall asleep I not be a burden to anyone" (Ign. *Rom.* 4:1–2).

The letters show that Ignatius anticipated later Christian orthodoxy in several important respects.

- He uses the term "catholic," in the sense of universal, of the church for the first time: "Wherever the bishop appears let the congregation be present; just as wherever Jesus Christ is, there is the catholic church" (Ign. *Smyrn.* 8:2).
- He advocates the hierarchy of ministry, the threefold office of clergy, that came to characterize the early church: The bishop has monarchical authority in his territory and must be present at the Eucharist. (Ignatius, however, reveals no trace of the later idea that the bishops are the successors of the apostles, from whom they derive their absolute authority.) The presbyters (elders) are the parish priests. And the deacons oversee the social work of the parish.

> Let all respect the deacons as Jesus Christ, even as the bishop is also a type of the Father, and the presbyters as the council of God and the college of Apostles. Without these the name of "church" is not given. (Ign. *Trall.* 3:1)
>
> See that you all follow the bishop, as Jesus Christ follows the Father, and the presbytery as if it were the Apostles. And reverence the deacons as the command of God. Let no one do any of the things appertaining to the church without the bishop. Let that be considered a valid Eucharist which is celebrated by the bishop or by one whom he appoints. (Ign. *Smyrn.* 8:1)

He who does anything without the knowledge of the bishop is serving the devil. (Ign. *Smyrn.* 9:1)

- Ignatius passionately attacks as heretical the idea that Jesus Christ was not a historically real person of flesh and blood, a doctrine known as docetism (Greek: *dokein,* "to seem," that is, "to seem to be human").

There are some who ignorantly deny him. . . . For what does anyone profit me if he praise me but blaspheme my Lord, and does not confess that he was clothed in flesh? But he who says this has denied him absolutely and is clothed with a corpse. (Ign. *Smyrn.* 5:1–2)

He is in truth of the family of David according to the flesh, God's son by the will and power of God, truly born of a virgin, baptized by John . . . , truly nailed to a tree in the flesh for our sakes under Pontius Pilate and Herod the Tetrarch. . . . (Ign. *Smyrn.* 1)

Be deaf therefore when anyone speaks to you apart from Jesus Christ, who was of the family of David, and of Mary, who was truly born, both ate and drank, was truly persecuted under Pontius Pilate, was truly crucified and died . . . who also was truly raised from the dead. . . . (Ign. *Trall.* 9)

- Ignatius unambiguously affirms the real presence of Christ in the Eucharist (Lord's Supper):

. . . Breaking one bread, which is the medicine of immortality, the antidote that we should not die but live forever in Jesus Christ. (Ign. *Eph.* 20:2)

The Eucharist is the flesh of our Savior Jesus Christ, who suffered for our sins, whom the Father raised up by his goodness. (Ign. *Smyrn.* 7:1)

- Although he alludes to Matthew and other New Testament writings, Ignatius's piety stands in the trajectory of Paul and John.

The goal of Christian redemption is personal immortality through mystical union with Christ.

Other Components of the Apostolic Fathers

Often also included among the Apostolic Fathers are 2 *Clement,* the *Epistle to Diognetus* (a later defense of Christianity to the pagans), and fragments (preserved by later Christian writers) attributed to Papias, bishop of Hierapolis in Phrygia in the early second century.

The Age of the Apostolic Fathers

The period 80–150 C.E. was a time of rapid growth of Christianity. By 100 C.E. Christianity was established around the eastern half of the Mediterranean; a bit later it had circled the entire sea. The most extensively Christianized area was Asia Minor, including the southern shore of the Black Sea.

The Apostolic Fathers as a group have a stronger interest in morality and worship than in theology. Wednesdays and Fridays were days of fasting. The Lord's Prayer was repeated three times a day. Worship services were conducted on Sundays. Divorce and remarriage were frowned on. In addition, there was a strong emphasis on social welfare, especially for fellow believers. Evidence exists of the growth of Christian conformity; norms and institutions were developing. Baptism was the sacrament of entrance, and all Christians celebrated the Eucharist, even though a consistent theology for each was not yet developed. Pauline and Johannine conceptions of union with Christ were no longer understood, and Christianity was seen as the one logical development of the Old Testament. The one exception—a most important one—is Ignatius.

No uniform doctrine of Jesus Christ (Christology) had yet been developed. Hermas could think of the preexistent Christ—the Holy Spirit—uniting with the man Jesus, while Ignatius could assert that the preexistent Logos (Word = Christ = Son) *became* flesh in a true incarnation. Such significant variations of belief left the door open for serious doctrinal conflicts, during which Christianity would develop from adolescence to early adulthood.

Conclusion

By the early part of the second century, it was becoming clear to Christians everywhere that they were something new, not another sect within Judaism. They could describe their movement variously as "the whole catholic church throughout the world,"[9] "the new people" that God had prepared for himself,[10] and "this new race or practice."[11] The New Testament itself makes the claim that this new people inherits the promises to the Old Testament patriarchs and that the words of the prophets and psalmists apply to Jesus and to them; these words were "written for our instruction."[12] Through conflict and trial something new had come into existence, but it still had to face a series of identity crises.

2

FROM VARIETY TO
ORTHODOXY AND HERESY
The Crisis of Self-Definition

Many . . . who profess to believe in Christ hold conflicting opinions
not only on small and trivial questions but also on some that are
great and important; on the nature, for instance, of God or of the
Lord Jesus Christ or of the Holy Spirit, and in addition on the
natures of those created beings, the dominions and the holy powers.
—Origen, *On First Principles*[1]

*The issue: How much diversity could the new religion tolerate, and
what criteria could be found to set limits?*

Dangerous as the external opposition to the early Christians could
be, internal tensions and dissension posed a more serious and constant threat to the survival of the new religion. From its very beginning, the church—with no developed and uniform system of
discipline or criteria by which to limit the variety of doctrines—
exhibited a wide diversity of beliefs and practices. In response to the
critical need for self-definition, the major churches and church leaders rather quickly—during the period 180–200 C.E.—arrived at a
rough consensus about (1) the components of Christian Scripture

(which excluded "heretical" gospels, letters, acts, and apocalypses), (2) a core statement of belief (resembling an early form of the Apostles' Creed), and (3) a line of authority reaching from the twelve apostles to the bishops of later centuries. With the definition of its canon, creed, and clergy, the church had become a self-conscious institution, with the means to draw a line between acceptable (orthodox or catholic) beliefs and practices and those considered heretical.

Early Christian Diversity

Whether there was in the first two centuries a normative form of Christianity—a system of beliefs and values generally accepted by believers in various parts of the Roman Empire—is a matter of considerable dispute.[2] To be sure, all Christians held beliefs about the significance of Jesus and shared common rites such as baptism and the Lord's Supper (Eucharist). Beyond that, however, they differed on serious and momentous questions: What is the relation between Judaism and Christianity? Must Christians adhere to the law of Moses? Do Christians follow the teachings of Jesus or do they center their attention on his incarnation, death, and resurrection? Was Jesus a real, historical human being or was he a phantom manifestation from the spirit world? Did Jesus speak for the Creator God of the Old Testament or for some other deity?

By the third century, as the new religion gained a strong sense of self, the concept of "orthodoxy" (from the Greek for "correct opinion") came to be used in opposition to "heresy" (from the Greek word that originally meant "individual choice" and later denoted a dissenting group or sect). When applied to the following groups of the first and second centuries, these terms are anachronisms, because the means by which to distinguish between "true" and "false" doctrine had not yet been established.[3]

The Ebionites

Descendants of original Jewish Christians in Palestine, this group eventually came to be considered heretical by church leaders. The Ebionites (the name is derived from the Hebrew word for "the poor") emphasized the ongoing validity of the law of Moses, reject-ed Paul's gospel of freedom from the law, and accepted only the Gospel of Matthew. Their aversion to bloody sacrifices led them to reject also the idea of Jesus' death as redemptive. For them, Jesus was the human son of Joseph and Mary upon whom the Holy Spirit descended in a unique way at his baptism. Jesus' main work was to reform the law of Moses and to give it is true interpretation. They called Jesus the "righteous one," the "servant of God," the one appointed to become the Messiah, whom God raised from the dead as a reward for his perfect life. Although such Jesus groups eventual-ly disappeared into the mists of history, they bequeathed to Chris-tianity many of its permanent institutions, including the rites of baptism and the Lord's Supper, other forms of worship, respect for history, and the tradition of social welfare.

The Montanists (New Prophecy)

The Montanist movement in the second century, also known as the New Prophecy, aimed at reforming the church by returning to its presumed original charismatic and moralistic character. The move-ment began in the 150s in Asia Minor near Phrygia when Montanus, a recently converted pagan priest, was suddenly seized by the Holy Spirit, fell into ecstasy, and spoke in tongues (from the Greek word *glossolalia,* which means "speaking in tongues"). He was soon fol-lowed by two women prophets, Prisca (or Priscilla) and Maximilla. The difficulty other church leaders had in finding ways to label Montanism a heretical movement can be sensed by the vituperation in an account written by a contemporary opponent:

> A recent convert named Montanus . . . was filled with excitement and suddenly fell into a kind of trance and unnatural ecstasy. He raved, and began to chatter and talk nonsense, prophesying in a way that conflicted with the practice of the church handed down generation by generation from the beginning. Of those who listened at that time to his sham utterances some were annoyed, regarding him as . . . a demoniac in the grip of a spirit of error. . . . Others were elated as if by the Holy Spirit or a prophetic gift. . . . Then he

secretly stirred up and inflamed minds closed to the true faith, raising up in this way two others—women whom he filled with the sham spirit, so that they chattered crazily, inopportunely, and wildly, like Montanus himself.[4]

The glossolalia of the three prophets soon changed into oracles given in the vernacular. These utterances were written down and gathered together by followers as sacred writings alongside of what is now in the New Testament. In these oracles Montanus used the first person pronoun for the words of God: "I am the Lord God almighty, transformed into a man." "No angel, no messenger is here, but I, the Lord, God the Father, have come myself." "I am the Father and the Son and the Paraclete" (in John 14:26 Jesus promises to send the Spirit, the "Paraclete," who would reveal all truths to the believers). As the movement grew, all sorts of minor prophets emerged with similar "revelations." For the Montanists, this charismatic outburst was a renewal of the enthusiasm of the earliest Christians, an invasion of the divine.

Along with the renewal of charismatic activity, the Montanists revived the primitive Christian expectation of the imminent end of the world. The various calamities—wars, plagues, famine—of the time of the reign of the emperor Marcus Aurelius (161–180) only stimulated such fervor. Montanist revelations predicted that the holy city of Jerusalem would shortly descend from heaven upon a reborn earth at Pepouza, a small town in Phrygia.[5]

Opponents of Montanism struggled to find ways to deal with this movement, the prime dangers of which were seen to be (1) the unpredictability of its revelations and (2) its challenge to the authority of the mainline bishops (all of whom were men). Not many Montanist claims could be condemned on the basis of Scripture or creed. The discussion therefore often degenerated into mere slander, as can be seen, for example, in what Hippolytus of Rome writes:

These [Phrygians] have been rendered victims of error from being previously captivated by [two] wretched women, called a certain Priscilla and Maximilla, whom they supposed [to be] prophetesses.

And they assert that into these the Paraclete Spirit [see John 14:26] had departed; and before them, they in like manner considered Montanus as a prophet. And being in possession of an infinite number of their books [the Phrygians] are overrun with delusion; and they do not judge whatever statements are made by them according to reason; nor do they give heed to those who are competent to decide; but they are heedlessly swept onwards by the reliance which they place on these [imposters]. And they allege that they have learned something more through these than from the law, and prophets, and the Gospels. But they magnify these wretched women above the Apostles and every gift of grace so that some of them presume to assert that there is in them something superior to Christ. These acknowledge God to be the Father of the universe, and Creator of all things, similarly with the Church, and [receive] as many things as the Gospel testifies concerning Christ. They introduce, however, the novelties of fasts, and feasts, and meals of parched food, and repasts of radishes, alleging that they have been instructed by women. And some of these assent to the heresy of the Noetians and affirm that the Father himself is the Son, and that this [one] came under generation and suffering and death.[6]

In general, opponents of Montanism permanently affected Christianity by (1) pushing the second coming of Jesus into the future, (2) relegating prophecy to the past, and (3) emphasizing apostolic tradition for the interval between 1 and 2.

Because of its strict code of personal morality and its fervent piety, Montanism strongly appealed to the most devoted Christians. In the face of harsh opposition, it survived as a Christian sect until at least the fifth century.

Gnosticism

A collection of widely varying, amorphous, mystical, religious-philosophical groups in the first three centuries, Gnosticism is notoriously difficult to define. Some scholars have seen it as the "acute Hellenizing of Christianity"—the mixing of Greek philosophical and religious ideas with original Christian beliefs[7]—others as a pre-Christian religious system, others as a Christian heresy that drew on elements from a wide variety of religious and philosophical traditions. Elements common to most gnostic groups, however, show that it was a religion of personal redemption based on dualism (the belief in two eternal principles) and esoteric, mystical knowledge (*gnōsis* in Greek means "knowledge").

Gnostics assumed that this world is evil—for some, hell—and not the creation of the supreme God, who in Gnosticism remained completely unknowable apart from revelation. This world arose either from the actions of a lesser or hostile deity (for some, the God of the Old Testament) or from downward emanations ("archons," "planets," "heavens," demonic forces, or "authorities") from the realm of pure spirit. All humans have body and soul, and a few have also the "divine spark," a remnant of the spiritual world. Some people live according to the body; these are beyond the hope of redemption. Others live according to the soul; these—perhaps members of non-gnostic churches—have latent capacity for gnosis. The "spiritual" (*pneumatikoi*), members of gnostic sects, are "by nature" or "by origin" saved.[8]

Redemption involves knowledge (*gnōsis*) of the origin of the world and humanity and especially of the supreme God. Salvation is ascent to the upper, spiritual reality and ultimate union with the fullness of spiritual reality (the *plērōma*). If there is a redeemer figure in a gnostic group, the function is to reveal, to teach—not to die a humiliating death and to rise again from the tomb. Christian gnostics therefore generally denied the reality of Jesus' death and resurrection—and of his human body.

Gnostic contempt for this world resulted in moral extremes. Some gnostics were acutely world-denying and ascetic while others allowed and encouraged libertinism, on the grounds that the flesh counts for nothing.

Among noteworthy figures in the story of Gnosticism are the following:

- Simon Magus was proclaimed by Justin Martyr (ca. 140) as the founder of Gnosticism.[9] Acts 8:9–24 describes the curious interchange between the former magician Simon and the apostles Philip and Peter in Samaria. "All" the people of Samaria, "from the least to the greatest, listened to him eagerly, saying, 'This man is the power of God that is called Great'" (Acts 8:10), which suggests that Simon presented himself as one of the major emanations from the spiritual realm. Later opponents of Gnosticism said that Simon identified his companion, Helena, as the Holy Spirit. Acts reports that Simon was baptized, indicating the relationship between Gnosticism and Christianity, but the story goes on to describe a repudiation of Simon by Peter.

- Menander was one of Simon's noteworthy disciples, but little is known of him. Perhaps a Jewish gnostic magician, he seems to have taught that he was the true revealer of the procedures that enable one to overcome the demonic angels that created this world and still hold humankind in slavery.

- Cerinthus, who lived in Ephesus toward the end of the first century, was probably the first gnostic to reinterpret the Christian gospel. He distinguished between Jesus and Christ: Jesus was the human son of Mary and Joseph, and Christ was the divine being that descended on Jesus at his baptism. After Christ—a pure spirit, incapable of suffering and change—had completed his teaching mission on Earth, he abandoned Jesus to suffering and death. According to his opponents, Cerinthus taught that, after the general resurrection of the dead at the last days, there would be a thousand-year reign of Christ on Earth filled with banquets, drinking, and sexual pleasures. The Christian writer Irenaeus (ca. 185) asserts that the Apostle John, entering a bathhouse in Ephesus, saw Cerinthus inside and immediately turned and left, saying, "The enemy of truth is inside." Irenaeus's report that the Apostle John was the teacher of Polycarp, who was Irenaeus's teacher, is a claim of apostolic authority for his own antiheretical efforts.

- Satorninus, or Satornilus, of Antioch, a disciple of Menander, taught that the world was created by seven angels, one of which was the God of the Jews. The angels tried to make humans in the image of the supreme God, but failed. The supreme God in mercy gave the human who had been created a portion of eternal substance and later sent Christ to help humankind escape the slavery of matter, the chief symptom of which was human reproduction.

- Carpocrates seems to have lived in Alexandria ca. 130. He taught that the world was created by inferior spirits. Human souls are preexistent, and salvation consists in recalling that preexistence. Without this knowledge, humans are involved in a series of reincarnations. The Carpocratians, arguing that what is material is of no consequence, practiced free love, sometimes involving a community of women.

- Basilides flourished in Alexandria between 120 and 140. According to his teaching, 365 "heavens" emanate from the supreme God. The angels who created this world, one of which is the God of the Old Testament, dwell in the last of these heavens. Humans nonetheless have imprisoned within them fragments of the divine spirit. The Father sent his only begotten Son to rouse these spirits to remember these heavenly realities. This, however, did not involve suffering of the Son; Simon of Cyrene and not Jesus was crucified.

- Valentinus was perhaps the most influential of all gnostics. He moved from Alexandria to Rome ca. 136 C.E., where he lived for almost thirty years. Although Valentinus was expelled from the Roman church around the middle of the second century, he had many followers, some of whom were notable theologians. He taught an elaborate system of emanations (aeons) from the *plērōma* in a succession of fifteen pairs (syzygies). The last of the aeons is Sophia (wisdom), whose lapse led to the emergence of the demiurge, the God of the Old Testament who created the physical world. The aeon Christ, who was united with Jesus at his baptism, brought the "pneumatics" true knowledge (gnosis), while ordinary Christians are relegated to the middle realm of the demiurge. The rest of humanity is consigned to eternal perdition.

- Many other gnostic and quasi-gnostic groups existed as well. The Marcosians were followers of Valentinus's disciple Mark. The Ophites, whose name comes from the Greek *ophis*, or "serpent," venerated the serpent of Gen 3, who led humans to knowledge or gnosis. The Naassenes (from the Hebrew *nahash,* or "serpent"), the Cainites, and the Sethites also espoused gnostic beliefs.

Gnostics produced a large number of sacred writings, including gospels and treatises, about fifty-two texts of which were discovered at Nag Hammadi in Egypt in 1945. Among the best known of these are the *Gospel of Thomas,* which some scholars date as early as the first century; the *Gospel of Philip,* and the *Gospel of Truth,* possibly written by Valentinus himself.[10]

The gnostic movement as a whole presented a grave challenge to the other churches for three reasons. First, Gnosticism separated creation from redemption (the doctrine of salvation, at this time especially deliverance from death) by denying that the supreme God created the physical universe. In contrast, the early form of the Apostles' Creed rejects this idea by affirming that "God the Father almighty, creator of heaven and earth" is the Father of "Jesus Christ, his only Son." Second, as a corollary of its dualism, Gnosticism introduced a dichotomy between faith and history. Salvation takes place in the inner enlightenment of a human being by means of the gnosis that the redeemer reveals. Jesus is at times separated from Christ; in any case, the Christ has no human flesh and blood.[11] However, the early Christian creed opposes this by affirming the birth of "Jesus Christ our Lord" from the Virgin Mary and his actual suffering under Pontius Pilate, his death, and his burial. Third, Gnosticism cut Christianity off from its Jewish roots. Yahweh, the God of the Old Testament, was an inferior deity or perhaps an aeon or a demon. Jesus was the first to reveal the supreme God.

Marcion (second century C.E.)

Marcion and the churches he founded were one of the most serious rivals to "mainline" Christian groups in the mid-second century. The son of a bishop at Pontus (on the south shore of the Black Sea), Marcion was an energetic businessman who made a fortune in the shipping trade. Around 140 C.E. he joined the church at Rome, giving it a huge sum of money (200,000 sestertii, about $20,000). There Marcion developed his distinctive Christian theology and his canon of Christian Scripture—the first such list in church history. When the leaders of the Roman church learned of Marcion's idiosyncratic beliefs they excommunicated him and returned his money. Marcion then energetically began to found congregations organized on the pattern of other churches. He attracted many people, including a brilliant disciple, Apelles.

Marcion titled his major writing *Antitheses*[12]—appropriately indicating the dialectical nature of his theology, based as it was on contrasts between spirit and matter, Hebrew Scripture and Christian Scripture, God of justice and God of grace, law, and gospel. His point of departure is Paul's polemical letter to the Galatians. The radical contrast in Galatians between law and promise (gospel) led Marcion to postulate two gods. The character of law was for him incompatible with the idea of the good God, the Father of Jesus Christ. The God of the Old Testament, the demiurge, the God of the Jews, was the creator of the material world. Jesus was sent not by the demiurge but by the supreme God, who was totally unknown to humanity prior to Jesus. The supreme God appeared as man in Jesus, but without assuming a human body (Marcion had no birth stories of Jesus in his version of the gospel). This God became visible to human eyes at Capernaum, descending there in the fifteenth year of Tiberius (Luke 3:1). Jesus died not in the flesh but in appearance only. His resurrection marks the freeing of humankind from all obligations to the creator God. Jesus appeared once more—to Paul (at his conversion).

For Marcion, neither God has a beginning; there are two first principles. The demiurge, creator of the material world, is the God of justice—often harsh justice. The supreme God is the creator of the invisible world, characterized by goodness and grace. Tertullian, an important Latin theologian, said of Marcion, "The man of Pontus brings forth two gods: the one, our Creator, whom we cannot deny; the other his own, whom he cannot prove."[13]

Marcion encouraged an extremely ascetic life-style while maintaining some of the practices of the "mainline" churches. He condemned marriage and allowed baptism only to those who abstained from sexual activity (in that it was the inferior God who commanded humans to "be fruitful and multiply" [Gen 1:28]). While Marcion placed restrictions on who could be baptized, he retained the sacraments of baptism (with anointing and with the drinking of milk and honey to symbolize new birth). He also maintained the Lord's Supper, albeit with bread and water instead of bread and wine. His churches also had the common three offices of deacon, priest, and bishop. His dietary restrictions, however, included abstaining from eating flesh. In addition, he encouraged martyrdom. Marcion's opponents did not criticize him for his *practices,* even though they were based on his foundational dualism. Rather, it was his *beliefs* that they opposed.

One of Marcion's most original accomplishments was his conception of a canon of Christian Scripture for use in his congregations. (For Christians prior to Marcion, Scripture was the Greek translation of the Hebrew Bible, which Marcion rejected.) Marcion's canon had two parts: (1) *The Gospel,* a version of Luke shorter than what is now in the New Testament, which Marcion apparently edited to harmonize with his own doctrines, although it is possible that he used the form of Luke familiar to persons in his home area; and (2) *The Apostle,* ten letters attributed to Paul: Galatians, 1–2 Corinthians, Romans, 1–2 Thessalonians, Laodiceans (possibly Ephesians), Colossians, Philippians, and Philemon. Marcion's canon was undoubtedly a major impetus for other churches to determine which of the Christian writings should be accorded the status of Scripture.

Marcionite churches lasted for several centuries. Marcion's theology, however, involved two of the challenges raised by Gnosticism: the separation of redemption from creation and the separation of Christianity from its roots in Judaism.

The Church's Response: The Appeal to Apostolicity

Montanists, gnostics, and Marcion not only expounded values and teachings that seemed intolerable to many Christians, but they had their own sacred writings and appealed to the authority of the first generation of Christian leaders. Further complicating matters, during some persecutions Christians were asked to hand over their sacred books, but which books were too sacred to be treated so contemptuously? Could the various Christian groups come to a consensus on these matters? Gradually it became apparent to many Christians that the question of authority and diversity in the church involved three questions: (1) Which writings should be considered authoritative Scripture? (2) Which Christian beliefs are nonnegotiable? (3) Which persons or person in the church should have final authority to settle disputes? Rather quickly—between the years 180 and 200—there emerged in major Christian centers, including Rome, a consensus on these three questions. The common basis of this consensus was the concept of apostolic authority—apostolic writings, apostolic beliefs, and individuals to whom apostolic authority is transmitted in every age.

The Apostolic Canon

From the beginning, "the Scriptures" for followers of Jesus consisted of the Greek translation (the Septuagint) of what we call the Old Testament plus some books of the Apocrypha. The term "Scriptures" in the New Testament always refers to the Greek Old Testament. As Christian writings began to appear, some of them were read in Christian worship alongside Old Testament passages. By the middle of the second century, most churches were reading texts from the Gospels and also letters, such as those of Paul.

Marcion assembled the first Christian Scripture—a canon—by the middle of the second century. Other churches had to respond. Around 200, the Western churches had a New Testament canon, as evidenced by the Roman list known as the Muratorian Canon, which included the four Gospels plus Acts, all the letters of Paul (including 1–2 Timothy and Titus), Jude, 1–2 John, Revelation, and the *Apocalypse of Peter*. Certain books remained disputed; for example, Hebrews and Revelation were disputed in the East. General consensus on the list of New Testament books was reached by 200, even though the earliest list that corresponds exactly with the New Testament of today is in a letter of the theologian Athanasius in the year 367.

The formal criterion for determining the New Testament canon was apostolicity: Which books originated with an apostle, or a disciple of an apostle, or, at least, represent the teaching of the apostles? So, for example, the Gospels of Matthew and John were eventually attributed to the apostles of those names, while Mark was believed to have been a disciple of Peter and Luke of Paul. The actual factors involved in the process of canonization, however, were perhaps more practical: Which books were venerated by the majority of Christians and read by them in their worship services? At any rate, the major churches by 200 had rejected the gospels, acts, letters, and apocalypses of the groups that were coming to be considered sectarian or heretical.

The Apostolic Creed

From the beginning Christians made affirmations of belief on liturgical occasions such as baptism, exorcism, and celebrations of the Eucharist. An early form of the creed, a prototype of the Apostles' Creed so familiar yet today, was the Old Roman Creed used in the church at Rome by 200. It was a series of three questions, apparently addressed to candidates for baptism (catechumens):[14]

Do you believe in God the Father almighty?

Do you believe in Jesus Christ the Son of God, who was born of Holy Spirit and the Virgin Mary, who was crucified under Pontius Pilate, died, and rose the third day living from the dead, and ascended into heaven, and sat down at the right hand of the Father, and will come to judge the living and the dead?

Do you believe in the Holy Spirit, and the Holy Church, and the resurrection of the flesh?[15]

No one who denied the real humanity (fleshly body) of Jesus or who separated the Father of Jesus from the creator of the world could confess this creed with integrity. The Old Roman Creed was intended to exclude gnostics and all other docetists.

The Apostolic Clergy

Christians gradually developed their Scripture and their creed. But what should be done if a dispute arose that could not be settled on the basis of Scripture or creed? An example of such a dispute is the "Easter controversy" of the late second century. The churches of Asia Minor followed the Gospel of John in commemorating the death of Jesus on Nisan 14 in the Jewish calendar,[16] and Easter was two days later—no matter on what day of the week it fell. The Roman church generally followed Matthew, Mark, and Luke in dating the death of Jesus to Nisan 15, but it placed more emphasis on the resurrection than the cross and insisted on observing Easter always on Sunday. How could such a dispute be settled, when the apostolic Scriptures and the apostolic bishops disagreed among themselves? The Roman bishop Victor I, ca. 195, who was repulsed by the fact that some Roman Christians, of Eastern origin, perhaps, were celebrating Easter while others in Rome were fasting during Holy Week, simply excommunicated first the Asiatic group in Rome and then the churches of Asia Minor as a whole. This is the first recorded act of a Roman bishop presuming to exercise authority in an area outside of his own. (The excommunication was gradually regarded as lifted.)

Already in the early second century, Ignatius had passionately defended the idea of the bishop as monarch of the churches in his diocese. Toward the end of the century, Irenaeus of Lyons in Gaul, formerly of Asia Minor, argued that the apostles' teaching and authority were carefully handed down to their successors as bishops of Christian centers. These bishops, in turn, transmitted this teaching and authority to their successors. Apostolic authority, therefore, is located in the major bishoprics of Christendom. And, among the bishops of the worldwide church, the bishop of Rome, successor of Peter, to whom Jesus entrusted the "keys of the kingdom" (Matt 16:19), most faithfully preserves and represents apostolic authority on Earth. Irenaeus thus for the first time intentionally combines the ideas of the monarchical bishop, the apostolic succession of bishops, and the primacy of Rome. When disputes arise among the bishops, therefore, the bishop of Rome has final say.

By the year 200, the large churches of the Roman world had arrived at a self-conscious concept of orthodox belief and had formulated criteria to distinguish between acceptable and unacceptable belief and practice. These assumptions can be seen in the writings of two theologians who exemplify the tendencies of the Western (Latin) church and the Eastern (Greek) church, respectively, namely, Tertullian and Origen.

Tertullian (ca. 150–225)

Born to pagan parents in Carthage, North Africa, Tertullian studied law in Rome and then became a Christian in about 190. He returned to Carthage as a presbyter (from the Greek term for "elder"; the English word "priest" is derived from this Greek term). There he wrote a large number of books, many of them defending Christianity against paganism and also against "heresies" within the church, and others on all aspects of Christian ethics and manners. Well-read in philosophy and history and skilled in both Greek and Latin, Tertullian was the first major Christian writer to use Latin and to set the pattern for the precise, sometimes juridical, thought and language of Western theology.

Tertullian wrote in a vivid, compelling, and sometimes sarcastic style on a wide variety of topics, from speculation on the Trinity to women's cosmetics. Two of his comments have entered the ranks of familiar Christian quotations: "What indeed has Athens to do with Jerusalem? What concord is there between the Academy and the Church? What between heresies and Christians?"[17] And "The Son of God was crucified; I am not ashamed . . . of it. And the Son of God died; it is by all means to be believed, because it is absurd (*credendum quia absurdum est*). And he was buried, and rose again; the fact is certain, because it is impossible."[18] In spite of such rhetoric, which seems to be the opposite of apologists such as Justin, Tertullian was hardly irrational. He asserts that some things, like the crucifixion or baptism, are beyond understanding and that unrestrained speculation can lead a person far afield. What is important is God's revelation in Scripture.

The following is a summary of some of Tertullian's creative suggestions and themes.

- Tertullian anticipated the later Western doctrine of original sin, "an antecedent evil that arises from its corrupt origin." But grace, infused into a person, is "more potent than nature."[19]
- Baptism is initiation into the church and removes all previous sins. Tertullian therefore advised delaying baptism until the person is mature, usually not before marriage.
- For sins after baptism there must be satisfaction by voluntary ascetic practices. The more one punishes oneself, the less God will punish, said Tertullian. This is the concept of penance.
- In speculating about the Trinity and the relation between Jesus and God, Tertullian introduced two terms that have become classic, "substance" and "person." "Substance" is used in its legal sense: property and the right to use it. The emperor's substance is the empire, which he can share with his son. God is one in substance and three in person.
- Jesus the Christ is both human and divine but yet one in person. Tertullian had no patience with docetists, who denied the reality of Jesus' body.
- Religious authority, according to Tertullian, is to be found exclusively in the orthodox church, located there with the bishops.
- Other technical terms in Latin that Tertullian coined, and which were used by subsequent theologians include Trinity, sacrament, satisfaction, and merit.

Despite his anti-heretical fervor and his influence on later theology, Tertullian joined the Montanist movement ca. 207, largely because of its fervor and asceticism. He nonetheless is widely remembered as the father of Latin [Western] Christianity, the greatest theologian in the West until Augustine.

Origen (ca. 185–254)

One of the most brilliant persons in church history, Origen was born into a Christian family in about 185, probably at Alexandria, an intellectual and academic center of the eastern Mediterranean. When his father was killed during the persecution under the emperor Severus ca. 202, his mother hid Origen's clothing, thinking to deter her son from seeking the same fate. At about the age of twenty, ca. 203, Origen became the head of the Christian school at Alexandria, where he gained fame as a teacher. His moral seriousness and ascetic nature led him to emasculate himself to avoid the appearance of impropriety when dealing with inquirers into the faith.[20] He moved to Palestine in 215, later returned to Alexandria, and then, banished by his bishop, moved to Caesarea in Palestine. He died ca. 254 as a result of being tortured during the Decian persecutions.

Origen excelled in languages, textual criticism, biblical study, philosophy, Christian apologetics, and systematic theology, among other areas. The range of his scholarly production and the sheer volume of his writings, more of which have survived than from any other Christian writer before the Council of Nicea in 325, make it difficult to summarize without distortion:

- *Biblical scholarship.* Origen wrote extensive commentaries on almost every biblical book, including thirty-two "books" of commentary on the Gospel of John. He spent twenty-eight years compiling the *Hexapla,* the Old Testament in six columns: the Hebrew text, a Greek transliteration, and four Greek translations. Owing to the burdensome task of copying it, this huge project is no longer exant. Origen believed that the Greek translation of the Old Testament—the Septuagint—was verbally inspired by God. But it would be blasphemous to take every statement in it literally, such as anthropomorphisms and unfulfilled predictions. The Bible is meant for human salvation, and its interpretation must therefore be directed at the three components of human nature: (1) body—literal interpretation; (2) soul—moral interpretation; (3) spirit—mystic or ultimate theological interpretation.
- *Apologetics.* Origen defended Christianity in the face of attacks by the pagan Celsus (in his masterful *Against Celsus*).
- *Correspondence.* Only three of Origen's many letters have survived.
- *Practical writings.* Origen's writings on practical matters include, for example, a treatise on prayer and an exhortation to martyrdom.

- *Systematic theology.* Circa 225 Origen wrote the first full systematic theology in Christian history, titled in Greek *Peri Archōn* ("Concerning the 'Archons' or First Things" or "Beginnings" or "Principles"; translated into Latin as *De Principiis*).[21] *Peri Archōn* is a broad attempt to understand the inherited Christian message in a consistent system of thought—in this case, Platonism.

God for Origen is the only supreme and absolute being, self-complete, uncreated, and the origin of all things—including the devil. From this realm of spiritual completeness, the Logos—outward radiance and revelation—otherwise called "Wisdom," "Power," and "Son," that is, the preexistent Christ, was "eternally generated" (a phrase that would become important in the later Trinitarian controversy) from God.

Before the creation of the world, God created a finite number of "rational beings" or "souls" or "minds," all of which enjoyed free will, which is at the heart of Origen's thought. Also before creation, the Logos united with one of these souls—a sinless one, but identical with those that would form part of each human being. The "Son," therefore, although uncreated and sharing in the full essence of God, is inferior to the "Father," being derived from him. At the moment of Jesus' birth, this Logos plus soul joined the body of Jesus, which was derived from Mary. Jesus therefore had a fully human body and soul to which was added the unique Logos.

Also before creation, sin emerged among the preexistent souls by the wrong exercise of free will. Those whose sin was the least became angels; those whose sin was the most became demons and the devil; and those whose sin was intermediate were joined to human bodies at the time of their birth. The earth was created as the place where these fallen souls could, by faith and virtue, eventually regain their original status.

The Logos became man to effect the transformation of persons from human to divine, although the precise way this could happen is expressed variously by Origen. This process also, Origen thought, might involve reincarnations along the way to ultimate salvation. At any rate, given the continuing exercise of free will and an infinity of time, all will ultimately return to the condition of original blessedness—the restoration of all things, including the devil. God will then again be all in all. And then the entire world cycle might recur.

Origen's entire scholarly output had a tremendous influence, both negative and positive, on succeeding generations. His theology overcomes gnostic fatalism while accepting several gnostic premises. It provides a way of understanding original sin and suggests the meaning of earthly life as progress toward deification. But church politicians often disliked him, and his theological system could be criticized: It assumed that the entire course of human history is but the mending of a cosmic fault[22] and presupposed also a hierarchy of being and a mystical piety that were at odds with the more juridical thinking of the West. At the same time, his allegorical method of biblical interpretation can lead to highly subjective results. Origen's greatness, however, is beyond dispute.

Conclusion

All of the evidence suggests that Christianity by 200 C.E. was maturing, gaining permanent means of self-definition, and attracting talented and prominent people to its ranks. The appeal to apostolic authority, with the three hallmarks of canon, creed, and apostolic succession of bishops, was to remain a permanent feature of the Christian movement. The crisis created by the stimulus of dissident groups now considered heretics was no small impetus for this maturation.

3

FROM PERSECUTION AND CALUMNY TO STATE RELIGION

The Crisis of the State

The mighty victor Constantine, pre-eminent in every virtue that true religion can confer, with his son Crispus . . . reunited the Roman Empire into a single whole, bringing it all under their peaceful sway. . . . People had now lost all fear of their former oppressors; day after day they kept dazzling festival; light was everywhere, and those who once dared not look up greeted each other with smiling faces and shining eyes. They danced and sang in city and country alike, giving honor first of all to God our Sovereign Lord, as they had been instructed, and then to the pious emperor with his sons, so dear to God. Old troubles were forgotten, and all irreligion passed into oblivion.

—Eusebius of Caesarea, *History of the Church*[1]

The issue: What should be the attitude of Christians to the gaining of political power and to the ethos of the dominant culture?

The relation of Christianity to the broader society has been a critical and sometimes contentious issue in the entire history of the church. But seldom has the world witnessed such a reversal of status—from persecution to the prestige of being the favored religion of the state—as the church experienced in the fourth century. This epic event has influenced Christian thinking in foundational ways down to the present. The "Constantinian establishment" denotes the close relationship between church and state in Western civilization that began in the fourth century and continued more or less unabated until the modern period, typified in the disestablishment of religion embedded in the Constitution of the United States of 1789 (although the presumption of Christian hegemony would persist in the United States for at least two centuries beyond that date). This great reversal can be said to have inaugurated Christendom, the situation in which the Christian religion—its values, rituals, and tradition—was assumed to be the official religion of the West.[2]

As earliest Christianity grew, it gradually came to the notice of prominent Greeks and Romans, many of whom were not sympathetic to the new movement. Conversions often broke up families, and Christians declined to participate in some civic functions. To many, the new faith appeared to be a strange cult with weird teachings. To others it was a threat to political stability and conformity. External opposition to Christianity therefore took two major forms: (1) political repression through persecution and (2) intellectual-ideological attacks on the credibility of Christian beliefs.

The Persecutions

Not surprisingly, the first persecution of Christians came from Judaism. Christianity began as a Jewish sect making messianic claims for Jesus. As Christians increasingly brought Gentiles into their movement and criticized temple worship and the Torah, hostility on the part of some Jewish leaders grew. Christians, moreover, appropriated Jewish Scripture and interpreted it in their own way. As discussed in chapter 1 above, according to the book of Acts the first Christian martyr was Stephen, a leader of the Christian Hellenists in Jerusalem. Accused of speaking against the temple and the Torah, he was stoned to death outside the walls of Jerusalem (Acts 6–7). Jesus' brother James the Just was killed at the instigation of the high priest ca. 62–63. At some point near the end of the first century, Jewish leaders took steps to exclude Christians from participating in synagogue services.

Christianity emerged in the Roman Empire at a time of religious upheavals and a proliferation of cults. By ancient standards, Rome's attitude toward religious diversity was tolerant. Any group that did not threaten the unity of the empire and that recognized the authority of the emperor by participating in rites honoring him as divine was tolerated.

Judaism was tolerated as the ancient cult of a clearly defined people whom Rome allowed to retain their distinctive customs and law, provided that they recognized the sovereignty of the empire. It was a legal religion. As long as Christians appeared to be a Jewish sect, they too would enjoy freedom from interference. Paul ca. 55 C.E. had asserted that Roman authority was ordained of God and that the emperor embodied justice on earth (Rom 13:1–7).

Roman authorities, however, soon began to see a distinction between Jews and Christians. After the disastrous fire in the city of Rome in 64, Nero began the earliest recorded Roman persecution of Christians. The Roman historian Tacitus, in a passage of historical importance (*Annales* 15.44), described the situation thus:

Neither human resources nor imperial munificence nor appeasement of the gods eliminated the suspicions that the fire had been instigated. To suppress this rumor, Nero fabricated scapegoats—and punished with every refinement the notoriously depraved Christians (as they were popularly called). Their originator, Christ, had been executed in Tiberius's reign by the governor of Judea, Pontius Pilatus. But in spite of this temporary setback the deadly superstition had broken out afresh, not only in Judea (where the mischief had started) but even in Rome. All degraded and shameful practices collect and flourish in the capital.

First, Nero had self-acknowledged Christians arrested. Then, on their information, large numbers of others were condemned—not so much for arson as for hatred of the human race. Their deaths were made farcical. Dressed in wild animal's skins, they were torn to pieces by dogs or crucified or made into torches to be ignited after dark as substitutes for daylight. Nero provided his gardens for the spectacle and exhibited displays in the Circus, at which he mingled with the crowd—or stood in a chariot, dressed as a charioteer. Despite their guilt as Christians and the ruthless punishment it deserved, the victims were pitied. For it was felt that they were being sacrificed to one man's brutality rather than to the national interest.[3]

To justify this persecution, limited to the city of Rome, Nero accused the Christians of arson. By the time 1 Peter was written (perhaps ca. 90), the mere profession of Christianity was a cause for punishment ("persecution for the name"; see 1 Pet 4:16).

Sporadic and local persecutions would erupt from the time of Nero until the first empire-wide persecution of 249–251 C.E. Some Christians were killed and property confiscated toward the end of the reign of Domitian (81–96). Trajan (98–117) applied against the Christians a law against secret societies; during his reign Ignatius of Antioch and Simeon of Jerusalem (a relative of Jesus) were killed, along with a number of Christians in Bithynia. The cultured Stoic emperor Marcus Aurelius (161–180) instigated the policy of espionage and torture of Christians and referred to their "theatrical display" and "mere obstinacy" when being put to death.[4] In 177 he issued a rescript ordering the punishment of sects that caused disturbances by "exciting the ill-balanced minds of people . . . with new winds of doctrine."[5] Severe persecution, including the death of Pothinus, the ninety-year-old bishop of Lyons, took place in Lyons and Vienne (present-day France). The Christian writer Justin directed his defense of Christianity to Emperor Marcus Aurelius. Finally, Septimius Severus (181–211), thinking to stem the growth of Christianity, made baptism—the Christian initiation rite—a crime.

Among the causes of Roman persecution of the church, the most important seem to have been the feeling that Christianity weakened the fiber of the state by disallowing emperor worship, refusing military service, breaking up families by conversion, and perpetuating a general aloofness and flight from civic duties. That Christians rejected the traditional gods was also considered to be atheism by the populace. In addition, the closed celebrations of the Eucharist gave rise to slanders that Christians engaged in cannibalism and infanticide (eating the flesh of the Son of God), and in gross immorality (love feasts), or worshiped the head of an ass (a slander transferred from Jews to Christians).

Intellectual Attacks

As pagan intellectuals gradually became aware of Christian teachings, they began to respond with critiques that drew on the Greek intellectual heritage.

Celsus (second century C.E.)

The oldest known extensive pagan written response to Christianity is *True Discourse* (ca. 177–180) by the Platonist philosopher Celsus. Although the work as a whole is lost, much of the text can be reconstructed from the detailed rebuttal written by the great Christian scholar Origen ca. 248. Celsus impugned the moral character of Christians, whom he called bamboozlers of women, children, and slaves. Christians, he claimed, must be robbers because they receive such, a premise based on the notion that no honest person would willingly receive a known robber. Furthermore, there is, according to Celsus, no such thing as an ex-robber. Celsus did not believe that moral transformation could come by means of conversion.

Celsus ridiculed the biblical idea of creation. How could God number the days before creating the sun and moon (Gen 1)?

The Christian proclamation of redemption appeared to him incredible. Did God come to Earth? Why? To learn something about it? To set it right? Why not create a world that did not need to be redeemed? And if it were in need, why not come earlier? If God were to come to Earth, would God choose a backwater like Palestine?

Jesus, said Celsus, was the illegitimate son of Mary and a Roman soldier named Penthera (or Pandera, a corruption of *parthenos,* or "virgin"). Joseph cast Mary away and she took the child to Egypt, where he learned magic. On returning to Palestine, Jesus gathered eleven rascals, sent them out, and told them that if they got into trouble in one town they should run to the next. Jesus was betrayed by one of his disciples and crucified. The Christians said that he would rise from the dead, but who saw him risen? Only one crazy woman (he is referring to Mary Magdalene). Why did Christ not appear again to Pilate?

The Christians claimed that Jesus was divine because he predicted his death. But, Celsus asked, where are the predictions to be found? In the Gospels. And who wrote the Gospels? The disciples. And when? After the event. As for the miracles, other people can work them too. And what was miraculous about being clothed in purple, crowned with thorns, and given gall and vinegar to drink?

The Christians, said Celsus, claimed that God would judge the world and consume the wicked in fire. What a skillful cook he must be to be able to burn half the world without charring the rest![6]

Celsus's deepest criticism, however, was to ask what newness Christ has brought to the world. Have the demonic powers been conquered? Has evil been defeated? The world has not changed since the coming of Christ, and there is no sense even in trying to overcome evil. People should be obedient to the Roman rulers, because they at least have been able to bring some order to life. At bottom, therefore, Celsus feared that Christianity undermined the greatness of Rome, the only power able to prevent the world from falling into chaos.

Porphyry (ca. 232–303)

The neoplatonist philosopher Porphyry studied in Athens, taught in Sicily and Rome, and published a number of books on philosophy, astronomy, mathematics, grammar, and rhetoric. Among his works is *Against the Christians* (Greek: *Kata Christianōn*), which survives only in extracts in Christian works written to refute it. Unlike Celsus, Porphyry admired the teachings of Jesus, but had bitter scorn for the apostles and church leaders. He applied to the Bible a kind of historical criticism, arguing, for example, that the book of Daniel was not written at the time in which it is set and alleging inconsistencies in the Gospels.[7]

The Apologists

A significant group of Christian scholars known as the Apologists (from the Greek *apologia,* or "defense"), ca. 120–220, attempted to defend the Christian faith in the face of popular slanders and hostility from the state. The names of several are known to us: Justin Martyr, Aristides, Tatian, Athenagoras, Theophilus, Minucius Felix, along with the great theologians Tertullian and Origen, who wrote a refutation of Celsus. The Apologists pointed out common elements in Christianity and classical philosophy (monotheism, morality) while ridiculing pagan myths (following a long pattern of such on the part of Greek and Roman writers). And they presented Christianity as the fulfillment of what the best minds of paganism had longed for but could not reach.

One of the greatest of the Apologists was Justin Martyr (ca. 100–165). Born in Neapolis (Nablus, ancient Shechem) in Palestine, Justin entered a long search for truth by studying various philosophies—Stoicism, Aristotelianism, Pythagoreanism, and Platonism—and became a Christian after studying the Hebrew prophets. He taught in Ephesus and then in Rome, where he opened a school (Tatian was one of his famous students). He is remembered for three writings: *Apology I,* written ca. 153–155 and directed to the emperor Antoninus Pius and his sons, Marcus Aurelius and Lucius Verus; *Dialogue with Trypho the Jew,* written shortly thereafter; and *Apology II,* written ca. 161. Along with some of his disciples he was denounced as Christian and, having refused to sacrifice to pagan gods, was scourged and beheaded in 165.

Justin tirelessly refutes pagan accusations against Christians and demands legal proof of Christians' guilt for a specific crime before punishment be meted out. But there is no evidence that Justin's writings—dignified, reasonable, and effective though they be—were ever read by the emperor or other highly placed Roman leaders.

Justin viewed Christianity as the oldest, finest, truest, and most divine of the philosophies. For him the Christian message consisted in knowledge of God (including Christ), morality, and the hope of immortality. The historical Jesus is God's agent of revelation, but subordinate to God. Christ, however, is the preexistent Logos— God's expression, word, thought, and mind—who had a role in creation and redemption. Before the incarnation, certain humans had possessed "seeds of the Logos" and thereby had arrived at higher truth. These pagans, like Heraclitus, Socrates, and others, were "Christians before Christianity." It was the Logos who appeared to persons in the Old Testament and revealed truth to the prophets (the "Word [Logos] of the Lord came to . . ."). Now, however, the Logos has taken shape and become a man, God's "offspring," "child," and "only begotten Son." By means of the Logos concept—familiar to Greek philosophers and used by the author of the Gospel of John— Justin attempted to include noble pagans among the redeemed and also to hold to the divinity of Jesus and monotheism at the same time.

The Last Persecution and the Constantinian Settlement

As Christianity reached the end of its third century, its numbers, fervor, and hierarchical organization could not be ignored by the leaders of the Roman Empire, to whom the church often appeared to be a state within the state. With Roman leaders seemingly uncertain whether to fight or join the new religion, these years witnessed startling vacillations between merciless persecution and attempts to curry the favor of Christian leaders. A sketch of the major events indicates the contexts.

- 250, 257–260 C.E.: The emperors Decius and Valerian instigated the first empire-wide, systematic persecutions of the church. Among the thousands put to death was the Roman bishop Fabian (January 250). Origen died from torture. All Roman citizens were required to demonstrate their loyalty by sacrificing to the emperor—something that most Christians refused to do.
- 261: The emperor Gallienus issued the first rescript of toleration of the Christians, restoring church property to them. Peace between church and state prevailed until 303.

- 285: The emperor Diocletian moved his capital to the east (Nicomedia or Chalcedon in what is now northeast Turkey) for administrative purposes and defense against barbarian incursions from the north and east. He appointed Maximian as "Augustus" of the west (Rome). In 292 he appointed assistants, "Caesars," for each half: Galerius in the east and Constantius (father of Constantine) in the west.

- 303: Influenced by the anti-Christian Galerius, Diocletian issued three edicts of persecution, ordering churches to be destroyed and Scriptures burned. In 304 Galerius reluctantly sanctioned the death penalty, which was enforced according to the proclivities of the ruler (few executions took place in the west but in Syria much blood was shed). Diocletian abdicated in 305 and Constantine, in York, England, was crowned by his army as Caesar over Gaul, Spain, and Britain.

- 306: Death of Constantius. Constantine claimed the title Augustus of the west.

- 311: On his deathbed Galerius issued an edict of toleration, signed also by Constantine and Licinius, whom Galerius then made Caesar of the west.

- October 28, 312: In the Battle of the Milvian Bridge Constantine defeated Maxentius and captured Maximian, thus becoming the ruler of the western Roman Empire, with Licinius his sole rival.

- March 313: Constantine and Licinius issued the Edict of Milan, which assured Christians of toleration and restored their property.

- 323: Licinius died, and Constantine was recognized as the sole ruler of the entire Roman Empire. Edicts were now frequently issued that gave increasing privileges to the church.

- Circa 330: In order to protect the Danube from the barbarians more effectively (the Goths were then centered north of the Danube), Constantine moved the capital to Byzantium in the east, renaming it Constantinople (which evolved under the Muslims to Istanbul), thus beginning eleven centuries of the Byzantine [Roman] Empire.

Conclusion

Within a few years Christians underwent what was perhaps the most traumatic crisis in church history—the amazing transformation from an officially criminal society, membership in which brought the death penalty, to most favored status. The building of elaborate churches and their rich decoration began apace. The church became respectable. The unpredictability and the irony of the change are seldom fully grasped.[8]

The alliance of church and state—the "Constantinian settlement"—was to be the norm in Christian history from the fourth century up to the modern period. The crisis of the state received permanent and decisive resolution, but the power and authority newly gained by the church would prove to be a mixed blessing.

4

THE TRINITARIAN AND CHRISTOLOGICAL CONTROVERSIES

The Crisis of Monotheism

In agreement, therefore, with the holy fathers, we all unanimously teach that we should confess that our Lord Jesus Christ is one and the same Son, the same perfect in Godhead and the same perfect in manhood, truly God and truly man, the same of a rational soul and body, consubstantial with the Father in Godhead, and the same consubstantial with us in manhood, like us in all things except sin; begotten from the Father before the ages as regard his Godhead, and in the last days, the same, because of us and because of our salvation begotten from the Virgin Mary, the *Theotokos* (bearer or mother of God), as regards his manhood; one and the same Christ, Son, Lord, only begotten, made known in two natures without confusion, without change, without division, without separation. . . .

                        —The Definition of Chalcedon, 451 C.E.[1]

The issue: How could the uniqueness of Jesus be expressed in relation to the oneness of God, and how much diversity of opinion could be allowed on this question?

If Constantine had hoped that the Christian church could provide the means to unite an empire that had been engaged in civil war for two decades, he was certainly taken aback to learn that the church, precisely when he gained firm control over the entire empire, was itself threatened with serious schism. It was a theological crisis, at the heart of which was the relationship between the polytheism of paganism[2] and the one God of monotheism.

The dispute broke out ca. 318 in Alexandria between the priest Arius (hence the term "Arian controversy") and his bishop, Alexander. Arius was held in high repute by Egyptian Christians as a venerable man of piety and learning. He taught that the Logos—the divine aspect of the Christ—was not eternal but rather the first creation of God, created out of nothing, the "firstborn of all creation," and therefore not of the same "substance" or "being" as God. In the birth of Jesus, this Logos entered a human body, fulfilling the place and functions of the "soul" or "mind" in other human beings. This made Jesus neither fully God nor fully human but something in between, a "tertium quid."

The Trinitarian controversy, therefore, centered on the question of the relationship between Jesus and God or, more precisely, the relationship between the Logos and God. In other words: How can monotheism be maintained if Jesus is divine?

The Council of Nicea in 325 settled that issue (but not to the satisfaction of everyone) without dealing with the next matter: How can one person, Jesus, be understood to have both full humanity and full divinity? What is the relationship within Jesus Christ of these two aspects? Such questions are the subject of the christological controversies.

The Prehistory of the Controversies

The earliest Christians, including the New Testament writers, were more concerned about the function of Jesus—what his life, death, and resurrection accomplished—than with speculation about his metaphysical nature. As the decades passed, however, many of the leading thinkers in the churches became aware of the need for

Christians strenuously to preserve monotheism—which was a strong attraction for persons living in a pagan milieu—while they were venerating Jesus Christ as a divine being. How could this be conceived? Consider the options under discussion ca. 200 C.E.

Most Christian theologians at the end of the second century used the term Logos, derived from the Gospel of John (1:1, 14) to denote the divinity and preexistence of Jesus. It was, however, understood in various ways. Tertullian thought of God as one in "substance" while three in "person"—Father, Logos, Spirit. Origen spoke of three "substances" (Greek: *hypostaseis*), the Logos being "eternally generated" ("begotten" or derived) from God. At this time in Rome the theologian Hippolytus viewed the Logos as changing in the incarnation, and Bishop Kallistos (Callistus) stated that the Father and the Logos were names of "one indivisible Spirit." Clarity was obviously called for.

Opponents of the Logos doctrine who emphasized monotheism at all costs came to be known as Monarchians (the term means "one ruler," namely, God). They accomplished their objective, however, in opposite ways.

The Dynamic Monarchians asserted that Jesus was Son of God by adoption. A certain Theodotus the Tanner came to Rome at the turn of the century and taught that Jesus became the adopted Son of God when the Holy Spirit entered into him at his baptism ("You are my Son . . . today I have begotten you"; Luke 3:22, variant). Similar to the views of Hermas, the Holy Spirit for Theodotus was the preexistent Christ.

The most famous of the Dynamic Monarchians was Paul of Samosata (ca. 260), who was bishop of the important Christian center of Antioch. For him, God is "one person," and the Logos is simply an impersonal attribute of God, which inspired Moses and the prophets. Jesus was a man—unique, because born of a virgin—filled with the power of God, that is, the Logos, in the same way but to a greater degree than other persons of God. Jesus was united by will to God—an inseparable union, but a moral one, not a metaphysical one. When Jesus rose from the dead God elevated him into something like divinity. But, as with Theodotus, monotheism was preserved at the expense of the full divinity of Jesus. Paul of Samosata was condemned by more than one church meeting (synod).

The Modalistic Monarchians preserved monotheism in precisely the opposite way, by asserting that the Father, Logos, and Spirit were three different names for the one God, designating different functions. Representatives of this position include Noetus (ca. 200), who argued that Christ is the Father himself, who was born and died, and Praxeas (ca. 200), who maintained that through the assumption of flesh, God made himself into the Son; the Logos is no "substance" but only sound and word. Tertullian quipped that "Praxeas did a twofold service for the devil in Rome: He drove away prophecy and brought in heresy. He put to flight the Holy Spirit and crucified the Father."[3]

The most prominent Modalist was Sabellius (ca. 215), who claimed that Jesus, God the Father, and the Spirit are one and the same, three faces or masks (Greek: *prosōpa*, "face" or "person") of God. As Father, God is the Old Testament lawgiver; as Son, the incarnate one; as Spirit, the inspirer of the apostles. Here there is no place for subordination within the Godhead. Sabellius's opponents argued that if the Godhead is purely and simply one, then it is correct to say that the Father suffered on the cross; Sabellians were therefore called Patripassians (Father-sufferers). But the emphasis on coequality and denial of subordination had an influence on the final settlement of the Trinitarian controversy.

Arianism and the Council of Nicea

The dispute that the aged priest Arius stirred up spread rapidly over much of Christianity in the eastern Mediterranean. Processions of priests appeared in Alexandria chanting, "There was when he was not," meaning that the Logos was created by God out of nothing and that there was a time when the Logos did not exist. Both Arians and their opponents skimmed the writings of the great Origen to find support. But Origen had been somewhat ambiguous: the Logos was eternally generated from God but subordinate to God. The right-wing Origenists leaned toward Modalism, the left-wingers toward subordination in the Godhead. When the New Testament could not resolve an issue, and church leaders were hopelessly divided, how could the matter be settled?

In earlier church disputes, Constantine had heard the case himself or referred it to the bishop of Rome or called a council of church leaders. The last was his course in this case. Constantine summoned the bishops of the entire Christian church to meet in Nicea (just across the Bosporus from Constantinople, then Byzantium). A large number—between two hundred and three hundred—gathered there in 325 in what is now considered the first ecumenical council of Christendom.

There were three persuasions among the gathered bishops: a group of thirty or so who insisted on a clear condemnation of Arianism (the deacon Athanasius of Alexandria was and remained the champion of this group), a similarly small group of convinced Arians, and the vast majority, who were not clear on the issue and simply wanted peace. Eusebius of Caesarea presented a creed for discussion; this was emended by the addition of two anti-Arian clauses and, under pressure from Constantine, adopted. The key terms in what has come to be known as the Nicene Creed are the assertions that the Logos is "of the same essence" (or "substance" or "being"; Greek: *homoousios*) as the Father, "God of God . . . true God of true God . . . and became human. . . ."

The council promulgated the creed, but to get it generally accepted depended on the attitude of local church leaders. The creed was criticized for its nonscriptural language (the word *homoousios* is not in the Bible), its novelty (we might say its modernism), and for its supposed Modalistic tendencies. Many moderate Origenists preferred the word *homoiousios* (similar essence), but this was strenuously opposed by the champion of Nicene orthodoxy, Athanasius of Alexandria, who was banished five times during the controversy that ensued. Ultimately, however, the creed was reaffirmed, probably with some revisions, at the Council of Ephesus in 381 and finally at the Council of Chalcedon in 451.

The Nicene Creed rejected a remnant of paganism in the church; Christ is not to be considered one of many half-gods or heroes or emanations from the Supreme Being. He is of the same essence as the Father. As if the term *homoousios* were not enough, the council added anathemas to condemn the distinctive teachings of the Arians. Ambiguities remained in conceiving the relation of the Father to the Godhead, and in the issues taken up in the christological controversies. Especially noteworthy is the fact that the decisions were largely negative in form—asserting what is not to be confessed while not explaining precisely how the Trinity can be grasped intellectually. Not least in importance were the political precedents: (1) the unity of the Christian church was now based on the majority opinion of the bishops and (2) the church had now become inextricably linked with the political power of state; Constantine, although not dictating the results, had convened the council and took a close interest in the proceedings.

The Christological Controversies

If the Nicene Creed affirmed the full divinity and humanity of Jesus Christ, the christological controversies centered on the question of how one person, Jesus, could be thought of as both God and man. Could Jesus on Earth get sick? Tired? Could he sin? Was he omniscient? What did it mean that he could pray, "Not what I want, but what you want" (Mark 14:36), or that he could say, "Now my soul (*psyche*) is troubled" (John 12:27) or that not "the Son" but only the Father knew the time of the end (Mark 13:32)? Did Jesus Christ have two natures? Two wills? Two souls?

It was no longer admissible to deny the full divinity of Christ. But two options remained open:

* The unity of Christ—one consciousness, will, personal center— could be emphasized. This unity—the Logos—was united with the flesh to form the person of Jesus. According to this view, typical of Alexandrian theologians such as Apollinarius (d. ca. 392), the Logos took the place in Jesus that the "soul" has in all other human beings. Jesus had no human mind or will. The effect of

this approach was to minimize or deny the real humanness of Jesus.

- The completeness and integrity of Jesus' two natures could be affirmed, such that in the incarnation the Logos was joined to a complete human being, with a human body and "soul" or "mind." Such a view was typical of scholars at Antioch, the most influential of whom was Nestorius, who became bishop of Constantinople. Nestorius created a storm of controversy when he argued that Mary should be venerated not as *Theotokos* (Mother of God or Bearer of God) but as *Christotokos* (Mother of Christ or Bearer of Christ), because "that which is born of the flesh is flesh." Having touched on an element of popular piety, Nestorius was ultimately banished to the deserts of Egypt, where he died in the very year, 451, in which the controversy was—for practical purposes—settled.[4] For Nestorius and his colleagues, prominent among whom was Theodore of Mopsuestia (d. 428), Christ *must* have had a human soul. The problem was to conceive of the union of the two natures, which sometimes was compared to the union of two in a marriage.

In 430 a synod in Rome called by the bishop Celestius insisted on calling Mary *Theotokos* and labeled Nestorius "the denier of God's birth." The emperor Theodosius convened the Council of Ephesus in 431, the effect of which was to increase hostilities between Alexandria and Antioch. Then, on June 13, 449, Leo I, generally recognized by Protestants as "the first pope," wrote a letter— "Tome"—in which he summarized the position of the Roman church on Christology, emphasizing two "full and complete natures" that "came together in one person." When the emperor Lucian convened the Council of Chalcedon in 451, the Trinitarian and christological controversies were "settled" for most Christians for all time (exceptions were the Coptic church of Egypt and its daughter, the Ethiopian church, and churches in parts of the East). The council condemned those who deny the title *Theotokos* to Mary and those who confuse the divine and human natures so that there is one will in Christ. Rejected also was any "confusion" of the properties of the two natures.

The upshot of Nicea and Chalcedon is that Jesus Christ must be considered a complete human being (human body and human "soul") to which was added the fully divine Logos.

Conclusion

Chalcedon is a watershed in the development of Christian orthodoxy, a huge victory for Rome (the decisions were framed in the words of Pope Leo I) and a lasting blow to the prestige of Alexandria and other Christian centers in the East. The Greek-speaking East had a long-standing suspicion of Christian leaders of the Latin West, especially Rome and the eastern tendency toward mystical piety stood in contrast to the Roman desire for precise definitions of doctrine. Doctrinal uniformity therefore could not be imposed on many in Egypt and Palestine who rejected Chalcedon (those who emphasized the one nature in Christ were known as Monophysites—"one nature"). In addition, the fracturing of the Eastern churches made it easier for Islam to conquer vast areas there, beginning in the seventh century.

Categories of Greek philosophy, which might pass in or out of fashion, were determinative in these controversies. The "Chalcedonian settlement," however, came to determine for most Christians the limits within which speculation about the relationship between Jesus and God could be tolerated. Unitarianism would be henceforth at least officially excluded. And for some, the passion of what Jesus taught would take second place in favor of dogmatics. Once again, crisis permanently shaped Christendom.

5

AUGUSTINE AND THE PELAGIAN CONTROVERSY

The Crisis of Salvation

Great are you, O Lord, and greatly to be praised; great is your power, and your wisdom infinite. And you would we praise, we, but particles of your creation; we, who bear about us our mortality, the witness of our sin, the witness that you resist the proud; yet would we praise you; we, but particles of your creation. You waken us to delight in your praise, for you made us for yourself, and our heart is restless until it finds its rest in you.

—Augustine, *The Confessions*[1]

The issue: Given the uniqueness of Jesus and his role in human salvation, how should human nature be understood, and how does redemption take place?

If the Councils of Nicea (325) and Chalcedon (451) determined for most Christians the limits of speculation about the relationship of Jesus to God, many foundational issues of the faith remained open and unresolved. Several of these are at the heart of the Pelagian, or soteriological (the word refers to the doctrine of salvation) controversy: What is Christian salvation exactly? How is Jesus effective in accomplishing it? What is wrong, if anything, in human nature? What is sin? Do human beings have free will in ultimate matters? How can we understand God's grace? And can human beings do good without divine assistance? The controversy over these questions was brought to a head by the mutually exclusive views of Augustine, on one side, and the theology attributed to the British monk Pelagius and his followers, on the other.

Soteriology Prior to Augustine

Although all New Testament writers presuppose that human salvation is somehow dependent on the work of Jesus, there is among these authors no single atonement theory or systematic discussion of free will and divine grace. That is, there is no uniform doctrine about what has gone wrong and how it is to be rectified.

In the Greek areas of the church (mainly the East), the emphasis was on human free will in matters of salvation. This was perhaps a reaction against Gnosticism and other beliefs that held to determinist thinking. Thus Origen insisted that human freedom is required to relieve God of being the source of evil. All human souls are preexistent; like all humans even now, these preexistent souls had free will. In a pre-cosmic fall, however, the preexistent souls, in varying degrees, sinned and therefore experienced the loss of God. In the birth of a human being, one of these sinning souls joins a human body (other souls became angels or demons). There is no room in Origen's system for the idea of inherited sin—as stemming from the sin of one man, Adam. Sin is due to the misuse of individual choice. Origen's thought does account for the universality of human sin: if you had not sinned in your preexistence, you would not be here on Earth, the purpose of which is to overcome the baleful results of pre-cosmic sin.

The Latin West tended toward the idea of inherited sin. This approach is suggested already by Irenaeus (ca. 130–200), bishop of Lyons, whose theory that Christ "recapitulates" in reverse the work of Adam implies the unity of all human beings in Adam. More explicit are the statements of Tertullian: Human souls are not preexistent but, like the body, come from the parents (this view is sometimes called traducianism). All humans therefore ultimately derive from Adam. Although technically free beings, human nature includes a tendency to sin—an "antecedent evil" in the soul that is "second nature" to us. The sin of the first man "infected the whole race by his seed, making it a channel of damnation."[2] Tertullian could call this "original vice" and identify it with sexuality. And so, even children born of Christians are impure until they are reborn of water and the Spirit.

In the Pelagian controversy, the Pelagians brought the Eastern teaching to its peak, while Augustine systematized the Western.

Augustine (354–430)

Often considered the greatest early Christian leader up to this time, Augustine left a permanent imprint on subsequent Christianity, especially in the West. He was born to a Christian mother, Monica, and a pagan father, Patricius (who was baptized shortly before his death, ca. 370), at Tagaste in Numidia, North Africa, on November 13, 354. Because of his autobiography, *Confessions,* written shortly before 400, his life, both external and internal, is better known to us than that of any other ancient Christian. Entirely in the form of a prayer to God, the *Confessions* recounts his life through his conversion to Christianity in 386.

Unbaptized as a child, Augustine received early Christian influence from his mother, while his father encouraged the study of Greek and Roman classics, from which he gained a passion for the question of truth. While studying rhetoric at Carthage, Augustine took a mistress, to whom he was faithful for fifteen years and with whom he had a beloved son, Adeotatus, who died in 389 at the age of seventeen. Also, it was probably during his time at Carthage that Augustine became a Manichaean.[3] However, he quit the movement after nine years. Shortly after 383, Augustine moved to Rome where he founded a school of rhetoric but, revulsed by the immoral behavior of his students, accepted a teaching position in Milan, where he soon came under the influence of Ambrose. He became a neoplatonist,[4] while at the same time moving toward Christianity. As he had been attracted to the asceticism and strict morality of the Manichaeans, he had the highest respect for the asceticism of Christian monks and saints.

Torn between the dualism of the Manichaeans and the monism of neoplatonism, between his own lifestyle and that of the ascetics, and between a passion for truth and the experience of skepticism, Augustine converted to Christianity one day in Milan in 386 when, sitting in a garden, he "heard from a neighboring house a voice, as of boy or girl, I know not, chanting, and oft repeating, 'Take up and read; Take up and read.'" He picked up the book at hand and opened it to the first passage he found: Paul's words in Rom 13:13–14: "Not in reveling and drunkenness, not in debauchery and licentiousness, not in quarreling and jealousy. Instead, put on the Lord Jesus Christ, and make no provision for the flesh, to gratify its desires." The effect on Augustine was immediate: "No further would I read; nor needed I: for instantly at the end of this sentence, by a light as it were of serenity infused into my heart, all the darkness of doubt vanished away."[5]

Augustine's writings from the time of his conversion in 386 until his death in 430 are equivalent to approximately fifteen volumes in a standard encyclopedia. Several of these are often included among the great books of Western literature. Among these is the first philosophy of history ever written, *The City of God,* which was written in response to the fall of Rome in 410 to Alaric, a Visigoth king and Arian Christian. Augustine was especially concerned to show that the fall of Rome could not be charged to the neglect of the pagan gods on the part of the Christians nor to Christian neglect of civic duties. Parts 1–2 deal with the pagan gods, summarizing their ineffectiveness and absurdities. Parts 3–5 present the sweep of human history as the relationship between two "cities," the earthly city and the heavenly city. These are two kinds of humanity, two loves (love of God to the point of self-contempt and love of self to the point of contempt of God), two kingdoms (God and the devil), and two principles in time (truth, goodness, and peace in conrast to error, disorder, and confusion). The city of God is not the church as such but exemplifies the church, as the Roman Empire exemplifies the earthly city. God intends history to be the struggle between these two: the earthly city will suffer vicissitudes and setbacks, while the city of God will increase. Although Augustine in *The City of God* did not envision a kind of Christian theocracy on Earth, this work was adduced in support of such ideas in medieval times.

Augustine's views relevant to the Pelagian controversy, that is, on sin and grace, stem from the basic ideas that everything good—including faith—comes from God and that humans beings are not free; one cannot completely escape one's past. Hope for human salvation depends entirely on God's initiative. The corollary is predestination, an idea that Augustine defends. Details can be sketched:

- As shown by life experience, the human being is a "mass of sin" (*massa peccati*). The result is death and an unbridgeable gulf between the human and God.
- Sin (evil) is not nonbeing but the turn from God to nothingness. It is an inherited condition, "the wretched necessity of being unable to refrain from sinning." This condition manifests itself as (1) pride, the sin of the soul, and (2) concupiscence, the downward pull of the body, associated with the lust of the flesh.
- The wages of sin is death, both physical and spiritual. If Adam had not sinned he would have lived forever.
- Before Adam sinned he had free will, which was influenced in the direction of God. Otherwise he would not have been able to sin. All subsequent sins of humanity, however, are caused by the corruption of human nature in the sin of Adam.
- Every person is born with original sin, a kind of sexually transmitted disease. Adam's fall corrupted human nature, and all subsequent persons are born in a state of condemnation and with a tendency to commit sin. This view necessitates infant baptism, which removes the guilt of original sin but not the tendency to commit sin.
- The only hope human beings have for salvation is God's sheer grace. This grace is prevenient, that is, God must create faith in the human heart so that it can receive this grace. Humans cannot even choose to believe.

- Because experience shows that not all persons receive grace, it necessarily follows that God gives grace only to those whom he chooses; thus predestination. Augustine goes so far as to speak of a "fixed number of the elect" who will enter eternal life and those who will be eternally damned.
- The human being is therefore justified by faith through grace. Justification not only removes guilt but also gives one power to do good.
- Sanctification is the gaining of merit in the sight of God by acts of faith, hope, and love and the taking on of more than what is required (the "counsel of the gospel").

The Pelagians

Pelagius was a British monk who came to Rome shortly after 400 and was shocked by the immorality he found there, even among clergy. Roman church leaders excused such behavior by referring to the hardness of God's demands and the frailty of the flesh. Circa 410 Augustine received the news that Pelagius was criticizing a sentence in Augstine's *Confessions,* "Give what you command, and command what you will" (10.29),[6] which seemed to suggest that human ability to do good and refrain from evil was possible only by the gift of God's grace. Although Pelagius was unsuccessful in making personal contact with Augustine, a fierce controversy nonetheless took place by means of letters, essays, and disputes between their respective followers.

Despite the difficulty in distinguishing the teachings of Pelagius from those of his followers, it is clear that Pelagius had two basic emphases. First, God makes no impossible demands on human beings. If it were otherwise, God would be cruel and unjust or ignorant of human ability. Second, human beings have free will and are responsible for their actions. They are born without vice or virtue, capable of either. There is no original sin; it would be monstrous to think that God would forgive you your own sins and yet impute to you the guilt of someone else's sin.

The Pelagians taught that because God is both just and good, everything God creates is good, including marriage, the law, free will, and human nature. Evil is to choose what God forbids; it cannot be inherited. It is always therefore theoretically possible for a person to be sinless, although Adam introduced sin into our environment—a kind of baleful peer pressure. All humans are born into the world with precisely the same nature as Adam's at creation. The difficulty for the Pelagians was to formulate a clear concept of God's grace, which usually centered on the ideas of illumination, exhortation, and education.

The controversy was difficult to settle, partly because Pelagius's views represented the main line of Christian tradition while Augustine was an innovator.[7] The Council of Ephesus in 431 nevertheless officially condemned the Pelagians. But the traditional settlement of the controversy is taken to be the decisions made by a local Synod of Orange convened by Caesarius, the bishop of Arles, in 529, whose views were endorsed by Pope Boniface II in 532. This synod attempted a compromise between what are arguably mutually exclusive positions: original sin was upheld; human freedom was severely distorted in Adam's fall; and all good work is the work of God. God's grace is especially tied to the sacraments; this enables one to do good works, which result in merit. Nonetheless, the idea that God predestines some to eternal damnation was condemned.

The central issues of the Pelagian controversy would break out afresh in the Protestant Reformation of the sixteenth century.

The Donatist Schism

A significant schism in the early church was occasioned by the question of what to do with those Christians who lapsed in the last great persecution, under the emperor Diocletian in the early years of the fourth century. The issue arose in the area of Carthage, North Africa, where the rigorist party in the church honored the idea of martyrdom and viewed flight from persecution or the handing over of sacred books as treachery that could not be forgiven. Moderates, led by the bishop Mensurius of Carthage, advocated prudence and were suspicious of the motives of the fanatics.

The issue came to a head when the persecutions ended in 311, when Caecilian was elected bishop of Carthage. The rigorists rejected his ordination as bishop, especially because the service was performed by a bishop named Felix, who had under pressure handed over sacred books to the pagan persecutors. Seventy Numidian bishops met at Carthage, deposed Caecilian, and elected a rival bishop, Majorinus. After Majorinus's death in 315, he was succeeded by the gifted Donatus, a man of fiery energy and eloquence who represented the legalistic fervor of early Christianity. Donatus was convinced that sacraments performed by an unworthy bishop were not valid, especially baptism and ordination, which were thought to leave indelible marks on the recipients.

Each party in the North African church tried to gain the support of the church at large. Donatists appealed to the emperor Constantine, who turned the matter over to the bishops of Gaul and Rome, who declared Caecilian the legitimate bishop of Carthage. Various appeals and decisions failed to end the schism, and some Donatists became ever more fanatical. The Donatist Schism lasted in North Africa until the Muslim conquests of the seventh century.

The underlying issue in the Donatist controvesy was the holiness of the church: Does it consist in the moral purity of its members or in the institution itself? More specifically, are the sacraments valid if they are performed by "unworthy" clergy?

Augustine became heavily involved in this dispute. He was pushed to the view that the holiness of the church does not depend on the holiness of its clergy; if it were otherwise, no one could be assured of eternal salvation. Sacraments performed by heretics or excommunicated priests are "valid," even if not "regular" and are not effective outside the church. Augustine's view on this matter persists to this day in the doctrine of major Christian traditions.

Conclusion

Augustine is one of the towering intellects of Western history, and certainly of church history. Although Augustinianism has more in common with Platonism than Aristotelianism, the great scholastic theologian Thomas Aquinas, an Aristotelian, quotes more often from Augustine than from any other theologian of the early church. Augustine's views on grace and predestination, honed in his conflict with the Pelagians, similarly had a great influence on the major Protestant reformers, especially Martin Luther and John Calvin. And Augustine's opinions in the Donatist controversy have determined the doctrine of ordination in Roman Catholic theology to the present day.

6

OLIGARCHY AND MONARCHY, EAST AND WEST

The Crisis of Authority

As God the Creator of the universe established "two great lights in the firmament of heaven, the greater light to rule the day and the lesser light to rule the night" [see Gen 1:16], so in the firmament of the universal church which is called by the name of heaven, God established two great dignities, the greater to bear rule over souls, corresponding to the day, and the lesser to rule over bodies, corresponding to the night. As the moon derives its light from the sun and is inferior both in quality and quantity, so the royal power derives the splendor of its dignity from the pontifical authority. . . .
—Pope Innocent III, *Sicut universitatis conditor,* 1198 C.E.[1]

The issue: How should the church be structured and governed, and where should its ultimate authority be located?

Momentous developments occurred in the seven hundred years from Augustine to the Crusades (ca. 400–1100). For example:

- The church spread rapidly throughout Europe.
- Christian monasticism took its permanent form and function.

- The church in the West assumed many functions earlier filled by the civil government, which collapsed in the early centuries of this period. The work of Gregory the Great (pope from 590 to 604) is significant here.
- The papacy evolved the explicit claim to have supremacy over all civil governments on Earth.
- The Eastern (Greek) empire reached its zenith, especially during the reign of the emperor Justinian (527–565).
- The Great Schism between the Eastern (Orthodox) and Western (Latin, Roman Catholic) churches took place in the year 1054.
- Beginning in the seventh century Islam conquered vast Christian regions, including the Middle East, North Africa, and Spain. By the eighth century Muslim armies had reached into France.

These several crises deal with a number of questions that involve the exercise of authority and power: What is the nature of the church? Who has supreme authority in the church? What is the relation between the church and the civil state?

The Rise of Monasticism

The emergence of a new class of Christians—monks and nuns[2]—in the church after 300 forced the church to clarify its understanding of its clergy and its moral standards, among other things.

Christian monasticism took root at the beginning of the fourth century in the areas where Gnosticism had flourished—Egypt and Syria. It can be understood as a reaction against the increasing power and worldliness of the church after Constantine and also as a substitute for martyrdom, which was no longer to be expected in a church-state system: "In the burning deserts and awful caverns of Egypt and Syria, amid the pains of self-torture, the mortification of natural desires, and relentless battles with hellish monsters, the ascetics now sought to win the crown of heavenly glory, which their predecessors in times of persecution had more quickly and easily gained by a bloody death."[3]

Christian monasticism, similar in many respects to that of pre-Christian Buddhism, latched onto and exaggerated ascetic tendencies in the earliest Christian writings. The earliest stage involved anchorites (from the Greek *anachōreō*, "to withdraw"), individuals who dropped out of society, choosing to live as hermits in the desert. For centuries individuals who fled the general society—to escape from debts, from enemies, or for some other reason—fled into the desert; this included Christians fleeing persecution. The biblical models for this practice were Elijah and John the Baptist. According to Jerome (ca. 342–420) the first Christian hermit was the half-legendary Paul of Thebes, who during the Decian persecution ca. 250 supposedly retreated to the Egyptian desert where he lived for ninety years, sustained by a spring and a palm tree and enjoying the company of wild beasts but no humans.

The historically demonstrable founder of anchorite monasticism, however, was Antony of Egypt (ca. 251–356), the "partriarch of the monks." Born into a wealthy Christian family, after the death of his parents in 270 he determined to follow Jesus' advice in Matt 19:21: "If you wish to be perfect, go, sell your possessions, and give the money to the poor, and you will have treasure in heaven; then come, follow me." Antony moved to the desert, living first in a tomb, then for twenty years in the ruins of a castle, and finally on Mount Colzim near the Red Sea. He spent his time weaving baskets, battling the devil and demons, and sometimes entertaining visitors. He ate once a day, after sunset: water, bread, and salt, and occasionally dates. In a move that was typical of monastic support for doctrinal orthodoxy, he appeared in Alexandria when about one hundred years old to battle the Arians. His biography, *The Life of Antony*, was written by the indefatigible defender of the Nicene Creed, Athanasius.

The potential for fanaticism in anchorite monasticism came to a head in the practice of the pillar saints, hermits who lived on a small platform on the top of a pillar in the desert. Their leading representative was Simeon Stylites (ca. 390–459), who spent thirty-six years on a series of three pillars about forty miles east of Antioch in Syria.

He wore a heavy chain around his neck so that he could never stand up straight; nor could he recline on the pillar, which was three feet in diameter. He converted thousands of curiosity seekers and called himself the "candle on a candlestick."[4]

The next stage of Christian monasticism was the cenobite life (from the Greek *koinos bios,* "common life"), the gathering of hermits into a cloister, with common devotions and manual labor. Monasticism in this form became available also to women.

Pachomius (ca. 292–379), a contemporary of Antony's, was the founder of cenobitism. Born into a pagan family, he served in a part of the Roman army that was opposed to Constantine. Through the kindness of Christians at Thebes, he became a Christian and, about 325, after Constantine's victories, Pachomius established a society of monks on an island in the Nile River at Tabennisi, about two hundred miles upstream from Lycopolis. He wrote a strict rule for his monastery, with a probation period, manual labor (boat building, agriculture, weaving), and a hierarchical structure. Before his death there were eight or nine cloisters (including one nunnery), with more than three thousand members; within one hundred years there were fifty thousand members. Legends about Pachomius and other desert saints began to accumulate.

Monasticism was supported by almost all church leaders and theologians, especially Athanasius, Basil the Great (330–379), Ambrose, Jerome (who wrote *The Life of St. Paul of Thebes*), and Augustine. Martin of Tours (d. 397) planted monasticism in France.

The leading monastic order in the West for several centuries emerged from the work of Benedict of Nursia (480–543). This patriarch of Western monks gave the movement a fixed and permanent form and made it useful to the church. A witness to the collapse of civil government in Italy, Benedict lived as a hermit for three years before founding the cloister of Monte Cassino in 529. (Midway between Rome and Naples, the buildings of the cloister were almost totally destroyed by Allied bombing in 1944.) This is the alma mater of the Benedictine order. Here Benedict worked for fourteen years, formulating the Benedictine Rule, which became the basis for all monastic rules of the West. The rule required the traditional vows—

personal poverty, chastity, obedience to the superior—plus the vow of *stabilitas,* remaining in the cloister in which the vows were taken, not being allowed to move from cloister to cloister. Benedict's rule was quickly adopted by existing monasteries, and new cloisters were formed as the church spread into barbarian areas.

A universal principle of monasticism was a distinction between the commands of the gospel, precepts that apply to all Christians, and the counsels of the gospel, optional forms of piety, such as monastic vows, that are taken by those who desire a higher degree of "perfection." The status of monastics within the church was an issue for a long time. They were the Christian nobility—the aristocracy but not the hierarchy of the church. Cloisters had long served as seminaries, and gradually—by the tenth century—monks were considered to be clergy.

Monasticism formed a functional counterpart to the corrupt life of the Roman Empire, providing an outlet for those weary of the world. It promoted the educational task of the church. But it also at times promoted indifference to family life and to service in the civil government. It fostered a kind of devotion that could become superstition (the cult of relics, miracles, veneration of saints, and so on), and the double standard of morality could have counterproductive effects. Its fostering of sexual celibacy also influenced the enforcing of celibacy of the clergy.

The Nature of the Church

By ca. 200 the Christians of a particular city regarded themselves as constituting a single community under one bishop, even though there might be several congregations. This is the concept of the diocese. At about the same time the clergy were beginning to be distinguished from the laity. By 250 the three major clerical orders (all male) were firmly established: (1) Bishops were nominated by the other clergy and then elected by the congregations in the diocese. Ordination was usually by a group of three other bishops. A bishop had supreme authority over his diocese. (2) Elders (congregational priests) were chosen and ordained by the local bishop, served as the bishop's advisors, and administered the sacraments. (3) Deacons were also chosen and ordained by the bishop and served as his assistants in the care of the poor, in administration, and in exercising discipline. Based on the pattern of Acts 6:5, the usual number of deacons was seven.

There also were minor orders. In the diocese of Rome ca. 250, for example, there were probably thirty thousand members, with about fifteen hundred widows and other needy persons supported by the church, in additon to forty-six elders, seven deacons, seven subdeacons, forty-two acolytes, fifty-two exorcists, some readers, and doorkeepers (who saw to it that only baptized persons remained for the celebration of the Eucharist).[5] There were also deaconesses, comprised largely of widows of clergy or wives of bishops; the Council of Chalcedon in 451 reduced the minimum age from sixty to forty.

The influence of monasticism was a powerful impetus toward requiring celibacy of the clergy. Most church leaders in both East and West considered virginity superior to marriage.[6] Church leaders had to argue that the Christian priesthood was not like that of Judaism, which was hereditary and therefore required marriage. The practice in the Eastern church was to allow one marriage to clergy, although the Council of Constantinople in 692 prohibited marriage to bishops while allowing it for elders and deacons. In the West by 400 all clergy were expected to be celibate, although priestly concubinage or secret marriages were common well into the Middle Ages, and popes themselves frequently had children.

Two competing conceptions of the church can be found in the writings from the early period of church history: (1) the earlier, purist view of the church as the communion of saints (fellowship of believers), and (2) the later view of the church as an institutional agency of salvation.

The earlier view was that the church is *one*, because all Christians are members of the one body of Christ and are also united in faith; *holy*, because it is the community in which the Holy Spirit operates and because all members are made holy by virtue of God's grace; *catholic* (universal), because Christians in all communities recognize one other as kin; and *apostolic,* because it holds to the faith and authority Jesus gave the Twelve. All of these terms were widely applied to the church by 200, and the Nicene Creed includes the words, "We believe in one holy catholic and apostolic church."

In response to controversies of the third century, an opposing concept of the church emerged—the church as an agency of salvation. Circa 220, the Roman bishop Callistus (Kallixtos) had already declared that the church could forgive persons guilty of grave offenses, because he as Roman bishop was the successor of Peter, to whom Jesus had given the "keys of the kingdom" (this is the first use of Matt 16:13–20 in connection with papal claims). The Roman church would later reassert its authority to forgive repentant Christians who had lapsed during persecution. Callistus also argued that the church is like Noah's ark, which included both clean and unclean animals. The church as "ark of salvation" involves the following ideas:

- The church is the institution in which salvation is reached. The classic definition came from the North African Cyprian (d. 258): "There is no salvation outside of the church" (*salus extra ecclesiam non est*).[7] In addition, "He who has not the church as mother cannot have God as Father."[8]
- The church is built on the bishops (the episcopate). According to Cyprian, "The bishop is in the church and the church is in the bishop, and if somebody is not with the bishop, he is not with the church."[9]
- The unity of the church consists in the unity of the bishops. Among these equal bishops, the bishop of Rome, "from which priestly unity has arisen, the womb and root of the catholic church," has primacy.
- The bishop is a priest who offers sacrifice to God, the repetition of Golgotha in the Eucharist.

The concept of the church as a mixed society on Earth was now official doctrine.

How the Roman Bishop Became Pope

Although most early Christians considered all bishops, at least in theory, to have equal dignity and authority, the bishops of prominent localities gradually came to be considered more prestigious than others. The hierarchy of the church evolved along the pattern of the structure of the empire: dioceses were grouped into districts, each headed by a metropolitan, and fourteen or fifteen districts were grouped into a prefecture. The main bishop of each prefecture was known in the East as patriarch. There were five patriarchs: the bishops of Jerusalem (honorary), Constantinople, Rome, Antioch, and Alexandria. The Eastern ideal was for the equality of patriarchs—oligarchy. The Eastern patriarchs therefore considered the bishop of Rome to be not only bishop but also the metropolitan of his district and the patriarch of the West. In the West, however, the monarchical idea prevailed, and the bishop of Rome rejected the self-designation "patriarch."

There were several significant stages in the development of papal claims:[10]

- Victor, Roman bishop ca. 195, excommunicated several bishops of Asia Minor in the "Easter controversy"—the first recorded such act by a Roman bishop.
- Circa 220, Callistus claimed, as bishop of Rome, to have inherited the "power of the keys" from Peter.
- Various synods and councils referred difficult decisions to Rome, which became the de facto appellate court in the church, especially in the West.
- Significant theologians, including Irenaeus, Tertullian, Hippolytus, and Cyprian, articulated the supremacy of the Roman bishop as an anti-heretical tactic.
- The first four ecumenical councils tended to accord to the Roman bishop first rank among the patriarchs, except that canon 28 of the Council of Chalcedon in 451 gave equal authority and prestige to the patriarch of Constantinople. (Rome never accepted canon 28.)

- The claims of the Roman bishops themselves were most decisive. Leo I (Roman bishop 440–461) explicitly articulated the claim that he had sovereign authority over all Christendom. The "rock" of Matt 16:18 is Peter, and on him the church is built. Jesus specifically entrusted him with the keys of the kingdom of heaven (Matt 16:13–20) and gave him the care of the sheep (John 21:15–17). Peter is therefore the prince and pastor of the whole church, and this authority is transmitted to Peter's successors, the bishops of Rome, the church that Peter founded. As Christ lives and speaks through Peter, so Peter lives and speaks through his successors. The bishopric of Constantinople, Leo asserts, is not founded by an apostle but has only a political basis. The Roman bishop, therefore, is the "first of all bishops," to whom is entrusted the "common guard of the universal church."[11]

By the middle of the fifth century, papal claims are explicit: the Roman bishop claimed supremacy over the worldwide church. But the pope did not yet claim supremacy over secular rulers, and papal claims continue to be rejected in the East.

The Great Schism

From the early decades of the church, the piety of Greek (Eastern) Christianity differed from that of the Latin (Western) Christianity. Already in the time of Tertullian the West traditionally sought precise definitions of theological concepts and operated with a juridical set of ideas that involved concepts of justification, penance, merit, predestination, original sin, and satisfaction. The cross of Jesus had a central role in this piety. Authority in the Western church was always hierarchical, and the church was perceived as a spiritual legal institution founded by Jesus Christ.

The piety of Origen and others in the East was more mystical and allegorical in tone, with much less emphasis on justification. They considered the church to be the mystical body of Christ rather than an institution of salvation, thus emphasizing the incarnation and resurrection of Christ perhaps more than the crucifixion. Sin was nonbeing, the diminution of essence, and salvation was rebirth and, at least for some Eastern theologians, apotheosis or divinization.

Differences between East and West, however, were political as well as theological. Constantine's move of the capital from Rome to Byzantium (Constantinople) ca. 330 was the beginning of more than seven hundred years of rival claims between the two centers.[12] In 395 the empire was divided between east and west, with the two sons of Theodosius becoming emperors. But the barbarians proved more dangerous to the West than to the East. Rome first fell to the "barbarian" Alaric in 410, and in 476—the traditional date for the end of the Roman Empire—the last Western emperor was deposed by the Ostrogoths. (The Eastern emperor retained nominal rule of the West, from Ravenna in Italy, but the de facto situation was often quite something else.) The lapse of imperial government in Rome had two important results for church history: (1) In the West the pope was left unchecked by a secular power, and the papacy often assumed functions normally filled by civil government. Eventually the pope would claim supremacy over all secular rulers. (2) In the East, now the center of gravity in the church, the ideal was harmony and balance between church and state. Often, however, the emperor exerted great influence on the church, a situation that westerners have sometimes called Caesaropapism (Caesar is pope).

One of the high points of the Byzantine (Eastern Roman) Empire was the reign of Justinian (527–565) and his empress Theodora. Justinian reconquered much of North Africa from the Vandals and Italy from the Ostrogoths. He was able to impose his will on the popes[13] and took measures against heretics and dissidents within his empire. He engaged in building projects throughout the empire, the most famous of which was the great church Hagia Sophia (Holy Wisdom) in Constantinople, the most splendid edifice in the world at the time of its dedication on Christmas Day, 537, and impressive yet today. (The Muslims on capturing Constantinople in 1453 made Hagia Sophia a mosque.) Justinian's most influential accomplishment, however, might be his codification of Roman law, the *Corpus Juris Civilis,* which regulated all aspects of civil and religious life and greatly influenced the development of the church's canon law.

The East-West differences in Christendom are exemplified in the "iconoclastic controversy" that convulsed the church in the eighth and ninth centuries. By 400, icons—flat pictures usually of oil paint on wood that represented Christ, angels, or saints—had become typical of Byzantine art and central to Eastern piety. Easterners considered icons to be channels of God's grace and of the saints' power. By the end of the seventh century, however, several influences hostile to veneration of icons were felt, including Islam. In 725, the emperor Leo III forbade the use of icons in worship, producing a revolt by monks and ordinary people. In 731, a Roman synod excommunicated the opponents of icons ("iconoclasts," or image breakers). Leo in turn removed Sicily from the control of the pope. A series of councils affirmed the use of icons, but the controversy was significant in the split between East and West.

Among the great theologians of the East is John of Damascus (ca. 675–749), who represented the Christians to the Muslim government of Syria. He strongly defended the use of icons, arguing that the image "is to the illiterate what a book is to the literate."

> The hill, Golgotha, the tomb, the stone, the very source of the resurrection—all are material; the ink and the pages of the Gospels . . . all are material. You must either forbid all respect to these things or you must allow with it respect to the images consecrated to the name of Christ and to his friends, the saints.[14]

John's most important writing is *The Fount of Wisdom,* a comprehensive treatment of philosophy, heresies, and the orthodox faith.

Doctrinal issues between East and West were never as significant as the political. The best example is the Western addition to the Nicene Creed of the filioque phrase: The Holy Spirit "proceeds from the Father *and the Son,*" an addition never accepted in the East. Western practices condemned by the East included fasting on Saturdays, the use of dairy products during Lent, priestly celibacy, and the rite of confirmation being restricted to bishops.

What is often considered the final split between East and West occurred when powerful men occupied both the papacy and the patriarchate of Constantinople. Pope Leo IX (1048–1054) meddled with Greek churches in Sicily, and the patriarch Michael Cerularius (1043–1058) closed Latin churches in his area, repeating old Eastern charges against Rome. Leo sent two legates to Constantinople in 1054, who laid a papal bull on the high altar of Hagia Sophia, excommunicating Michael Cerularius and all his followers: "Let them be anathema with all heretics . . . yes, with devils." Those who failed to acknowledge the supremacy of the papacy would be considered "an assembly of heretics, a conventicle of schismatics, a synagogue of Satan."[15] Michael in turn convened a council representing all Eastern Christendom that rejected the papal bull and condemned all who helped draw it up. The Great Schism remains in place yet today.

The Papacy Makes Its Ultimate Claims

In the period between Leo I (440–461) and Gregory VII (1073–1085) papal claims evolved from supremacy over the worldwide church to supremacy over both religious and secular authorities, that is, to world rulership. How did this happen?

No advance in papal claims was made by Gregory I, known as "the Great," who was pope from 590 to 604. The first monastic pope, Gregory was the most distinguished church leader in the West in this entire period. When Europe was in chaos, and serious persons thought the end of the world was at hand, Gregory took measures to alleviate starvation, began important missions, and expertly oversaw all aspects of the work of the church. Although the Gregorian chant is named for Gregory I, it is unclear what responsibility, if any, he had for its origins. We do know, however, that Gregory did distinguish between the eternal guilt of sin and its temporal punishment, making purgatory essential to the Roman Catholic faith.

The significant evolution of papal claims took place in part because of the relationship between the papacy and the Franks. The first Frankish king to embrace Roman Christianity was Clovis, of the Merovingian line, in 496. By the early eighth century, real power among the Franks was held by the "Mayors of the Palace," the Carolingian dynasty, especially Pepin (d. 714), Charles Martel (715–741), Pepin the Short (741–768), and Charles the Great (Charlemagne, 768–814). During the reigns of these four men, the papacy became inextricably involved in the succession of secular rule.

In 752, Pepin the Short forced the last Merovingian, Childeric III, to retire to a monastery and took for himself the title of king, being anointed by a bishop and subsequently by the pope. When the papacy was severely threatened by the Lombards from the north, the pope appealed urgently to Pepin for help. Pepin crossed the Alps in 755, defeated the Lombards, and gave the conquered territory to the pope. The Donation of Pepin marked the beginning of the Papal States, known also as the "patrimony of St. Peter." The pope now was also a civil ruler, a position that lasted until Victor Emanuel took possession of Rome in 1870 and reduced the Papal States to the area of the Vatican.

The reign of Charlemagne is one of the most striking and glorious events in Europe in the early Middle Ages. His goal was to unite all Teutonic and Latin peoples of Europe under his rule in close union with the spiritual rule of the pope. To this end he conducted fifty-three military campaigns, some to convert pagan peoples like the Saxons and others against Muslim threats. Charlemagne's rule extended from the Elbe to the Pyrenees and from Denmark to Rome. His zeal for Christianity was matched by his zeal for education. He founded many schools, required general education for male children, and imported scholars, chief of whom was the British Alcuin (ca. 732–804).

Charlemagne continued his father's protection of the pope and renewed the Papal States. In 799, Pope Leo III was assaulted and almost killed in a riot at Rome that was fomented by disgruntled relatives of his predecessor, Hadrain I. Leo appealed to Charlemagne, who came to Rome in 800 and helped to clear the pope of all charges brought against him by his enemies. In return, while Charlemagne was celebrating Christmas in St. Peter's Basilica, kneeling before the altar, Pope Leo III placed a golden crown on his head, and the audience welcomed him as "Charles Augustus . . . great and pacific emperor of the Romans!" This was the final papal declaration of independence from the Eastern emperor; the restoration of the western Roman Empire, later viewed as the beginning of the Holy Roman Empire; and the setting of the precedent that the pope has power to appoint secular rulers. Later popes would use this incident as a precedent for deposing kings and emperors.

Papal claims to secular control also stemmed from deceit. At some point in the ninth century a collection of documents falsely attributed to Isidore of Seville (d. 636) was drawn up in France. These false decretals or Pseudo-Isidorean Decretals contained forged letters of ante-Nicene popes, genuine canons of various church councils, and forged letters of popes from Sylvester I (314–335) to Gregory II (d. 731). Among these is the Donation of Constantine, in which Constantine purports to donate to Pope Sylvester I primacy over all Eastern patriarchs and civil dominion over all Italy. This document was used by various popes, including at the time of the Great Schism, but was demonstrated to be a forgery by Nicholas of Cusa, Lorenzo Valla, and others in the fifteenth century.

Further evolution occurred during the years 867–1049, when the papacy fell into decline, becoming the pawn of noble Roman families and even, at one time, being controlled by the prostitute Marozia. The buying of church offices was common, and other signs of moral decline were evident. Reform began in Burgundy at the monastery of Cluny. In 1049 the Cluniacs secured the papacy with the election of Leo IX, removed the election of popes from the Roman nobles to the college of cardinals, and prohibited lay investiture, the practice of secular rulers making church appointments. The dominant reform leader in Rome, Hildebrand, became Pope Gregory VII in 1073 and proceeded to issue the strongest claims for papal power yet made: the pope has authority to depose emperors and himself may be judged by no one. The Holy Roman Emperor at this time was Henry IV, who tested the pope's intentions by deliberately making an appointment to the archbishopric of Milan. The pope objected and many Germans denounced the pope. On February 22, 1076, the pope excommunicated the emperor and released all his subjects from their oaths—the boldest assertion of papal power to this date. The German nobles were split, and Henry was in danger of losing his throne. Henry decided to go to the pope before the pope could meet the German nobles. For three days Henry in repentance stood barefoot in the snow before the doors of the castle at Canossa, in the Alps. On January 28, 1077, the pope released Henry from excommunication. In later disputes, the emperor would be more successful. Henry invaded Italy in 1081; after three years Rome fell. Gregory VII went into exile and called in the Normans, who plundered Rome. The pope died in exile in May 1085.

In the Concordat of Worms in 1122, the successors of Henry and Gregory VII agreed to a compromise: the emperor would be present at the consecration of German bishops and princes and would grant them whatever secular authority they have; church authority, however, would be granted solely by the church.

The most powerful figure in the history of the papacy was Innocent III (1198–1216), who reasserted the claims made by Gregory VII, and who was completely successful in implementing them. He deposed the emperor in 1212, ordered King Philip II of France to take back his divorced wife, commanded King Alfonso IX of León to give up his marriage to a relative, and by excommunication forced King John of England to submit. In addition, Innocent III declared transubstantiation (the idea that the bread and wine of the Eucharist actually become in substance the true body and blood of Christ) a dogma and made provision for the Inquisition.

In his bull *Unam Sanctum,* Boniface VIII (1294–1303) attempted to state papal claims in even more grandiose fashion, arguing that it is necessary for salvation for every human being to be subject to the pope. When Philip the Fair of France, however, stopped clerical taxes from going to the papacy and the pope objected, the king took the pope prisoner, and the pope died one month later. For most of the fourteenth century the papacy became a French institution, with the popes residing in Avignon on the Rhone—in what has been called the Babylonian Captivity of the papacy (1309–1377).

Gregory XI, the last Frenchman elected pope (1370–1378), moved to Rome in 1377 and created a new college of cardinals. The cardinals in Avignon, however, refused these actions and elected

Urban VI as rival pope, creating the Great Papal Schism. How could such a situation be managed? Many in the church thought that the solution was to do what was done in the early church: convene a general council of bishops. At the Council of Pisa in 1409 both popes were deposed and Alexander V was elected. But neither of the other popes stepped down, and now there were three claimants. Finally, the emperor Sigismund called the Council of Constance, which in 1414–1418 ended the Great Papal Schism by electing Martin V.[16]

Conclusion

These various crises of the early Middle Ages generally persist to this day. The Great Schism is not overcome. Whether ordination has more than a functional character and whether it should be limited to celibate males is disputed. Whether the institutional church is more than the aggregate of congregations continues to stimulate discussion. And the authority of ecumenical councils relative to that of the papacy, whose ex cathedra pronouncements were declared infallible in 1870, continues to stir debate.

7

THE CRUSADES
The Crisis of Islam

The Saracens have recently reconquered the promised land. The king and his nobles are captive. The temple, the Holy Sepulchre, and the wood of the Holy Cross are in polluted hands. Because of our sins Palestine is given over to our enemies. The wrath of the Lord has descended upon Christians because they were unwilling to be one finger behind Saladin in riches. . . .

Besides, are the Saracens to be killed because God has given them Palestine? Does not God say, "I desire not the death of the sinner" [see Ezek 33:11]? The Saracens are men of like nature with ourselves. They may be repelled if they invade our territory, because force may be repelled by force, but the medicine is not to exceed the disease. They are to be smitten with the sword of the spirit that they may come voluntarily to the faith, because God hates forced service.

—Ralph Niger, *De Re Militare*[1]

The issue: How should the church respond to a new religion that conquered half of its territory?

Muhammad (570–632) and the Islamic Conquests

Along with Judaism and Christianity, from which it was influenced, Islam is one of the three monotheistic religions that sprang from the Semites. Within a century of the death of its founder, it had used the sword to seize control of Christian areas from Arabia to the border of India, much of the Levant, all of North Africa, a good amount of the Spanish peninsula, and southern France. The Muslims captured Constantinople in 1453, bringing the Byzantine Empire to an end. By all accounts this was one of the greatest disasters in Christian history.

Islam arose in the ancient Arabian city of Mecca at a time when its ruling class was pagan, even though the area had considerable minorities of Jews and Christians, many of whom had fled there as persecuted dissidents. In Mecca there had been for centuries a pagan shrine, the Kaaba (cube). In the northeast corner of the Kaaba there is still today a black stone, about six by eight inches, that has been an object of veneration since pre-Islamic times. Muhammad "cleansed" the Kaaba in 630 C.E. and surrounded it by a great mosque (Muslim sanctuary), making the city the most important pilgrimage objective for Muslims to the present day.

Muhammad was the ideal bedouin chief—of noble birth, handsome, imaginative, energetic, brave, and self-taught. His parents died when he was a child, and he was raised by his aged grandfather and his uncle. At the age of twenty-five he married a rich widow named Hadijah. It was a happy marriage, which lasted until Hadijah's death when she was sixty-five and Muhammad fifty.

In 610 C.E., at the age of forty, Muhammad, in a trance outside of Mecca, received his first revelation in the form of a call of the angel Gabriel, who in Islam often functions much the way the Holy Spirit functions in Christian tradition. Gabriel commanded him to "cry out in the name of the Lord." After a subsequent vision he began his life's work as a prophet who ultimately founded a new religion. Revelations came to him from time to time over a period of more than twenty years. Whether Muhammad was literate is debated; he dictated the Qur'an (Koran), the Islamic Scripture, to his disciples and clerks.

For three years Muhammad preached to family and friends, making some forty converts. He then began to preach to pilgrims coming to Mecca, attacking idolatry (polytheism, non-monotheism). Hostilities forced him to flee for his life from Mecca with his followers to Medina, a distance of some 250 miles north. This Hegira (flight) of June 622 C.E. is often considered the beginning of Islam.

In Medina Muhammad was recognized as a prophet and a lawgiver. He soon gathered an army and took the field against his enemies, gaining his first victory in 624. His conquest of several Jewish and Christian tribes in the area often involved massacres. The tribes that followed Muhammad, however, began to merge into a nation, united by common hatred of "the infidel," under the slogan "There is no God but Allah, and Muhammad is his prophet." The last section of the Qur'an commands the dispassionate extermination of all "idolaters" (non-monotheists) in Arabia unless they submit within four months.

In 632 Muhammad made his final pilgrimage to Mecca, with forty thousand Muslims. There he gave his final exhortation, planning a large military campaign against Greek Christendom. He died on June 8, 632, and was buried on the spot, now enclosed by a mosque.

Muhammad's successors, the caliphs, continued the use of the sword to extend their rule—with permanent and unspeakably tragic results for Christendom. Idolaters had to choose between Islam, slavery, and death. As monotheists, Jews and Christians often were allowed to purchase a limited kind of toleration by payment of tribute. Within twenty-one years of Muhammad's death, the Muslims ruled an area as large as that of the Roman Empire. They besieged Constantinople itself in 672–678 and again in 717–718, but the city withstood until 1453. In 707 all of North Africa—the home of Origen, Tertullian, and Augustine—fell. In 711 the Muslim armies crossed the Strait of Gibraltar into the Iberian Peninsula, establishing an independent caliphate at Cordoba. They crossed the Pyrenees into France, but were finally defeated by Charles Martel, grandfather of Charlemagne, in the Battle of Tours in 732. Over the next seven hundred years, the Christians of the Iberian Peninsula pushed the Muslims from the north to the south. During that time, Muslim culture on the peninsula flourished. And when the last Muslims were finally expelled from the peninsula by Ferdinand and Isabel in 1502 they left behind an illustrious history in art, science, philosophy, and other branches of scholarship.

Muslims claim that the archangel Gabriel inspired the Qur'an, which contains two kinds of revelation: (1) literal dictations by the archangel and (2) Muhammad's own inspired words. The Qur'an has 114 suras (sections) and 6,225 verses. Each sura except the ninth begins with the formula, "In the name of Allah, the compassionate, the merciful. . . ." It is written in pure Arabic, in poetic meter and much rhyme. The book, however, is fragmentary, and it is difficult to restore its parts to the chronological order in which they were composed.

The Qur'an is one of the classic books of humanity, a code of civil and religious law, with passages of religious fervor and wise counsel mixed with bombast and sensuality.[2] The revelations in the Qur'an often suggest knowledge of the floating traditions of Arabia and Syria, especially the fringe traditions of Judaism and Christianity. The Qur'an speaks highly of the Bible, "the book of God," "the word of God," "the Tourat [Torah]," "the Gospel."

Monotheism is the cornerstone and universal foundation of Islam. God is the object of awe and reverence, infinite power and sovereignty, and the source of fate. All humans owe Allah unconditional resignation (this is the general meaning of the word "Islam"). Prayer, fasting, and almsgiving are enjoined, while the consumption of pork and wine is strictly forbidden. Polygamy, slavery, and war against unbelievers are sanctioned by the Qur'an. Worship is severely iconoclastic, and Friday, the day of creation of humankind, is the sacred day.

The Qur'an refers to Jesus several times refers as "the Messiah Jesus son of Mary," and "the blessed son of Mary," but not as the Son of God, because God can have no wife. Several details about Jesus from Christian apocryphal legends are included. The crucifixion of Jesus is denied, and docetism is presumed to be common Christian belief. According to the Qur'an, Jesus predicted the coming of

Muhammad, the final prophet. Because the Qur'an includes beliefs about Jesus, Christian theologians into the Middle Ages considered Islam to be not a new religion but the major Christian heresy.

The Crusades

The loss of most of the territory held by Christians to Muslim armies in the century following the death of Muhammad in 632 was a devastating crisis for the church. The Eastern Roman Empire (the Byzantine Empire) faced a constant military threat, and Constantinople (Istanbul) finally succumbed to Muslim armies in 1453. Among all these tragedies, however, the piety of many Christians in the West was focused on the Holy Sepulchre in Jerusalem, the place of the burial and resurrection of Jesus, which had been in the hands of "nonbelievers" since the Arab Muslims captured it in 637. Although the Holy Sepulchre was the destination of pilgrims from Europe, it would be more than four centuries before a determined effort was made by European Christians to regain control of it.

Why did the Crusades begin when they did, at the end of the eleventh century?[3] A complex of religious, economic, and political factors came together.

- Islam at the time was divided between Arabs and Seljuk Turks. Europeans felt that recapturing the Holy Land was possible.
- Christian pilgrims had free access to Christians shrines in Jerusalem while it was controlled by Arabs. By 1084, however, the holy places fell into the hands of the Turks, whose policies were much less lenient and who showed little reverence for Christian relics. Reports from pilgrims such as Peter the Hermit about Europeans being brutalized on pilgrimages produced emotional reactions in the West.
- Europe had experienced forty-eight years of famine from 970 to 1095, with especially bad famine from 1085 to 1095. People were starving and looking for some sign of success.
- European kings had difficulty controlling unruly nobles and often were glad to send them off to the Holy Land.

- The Eastern church had formally split from the Western church in 1054. Many in Europe thought that crusades to Jerusalem might also lead to the reunification of Christendom.
- Crusades to recapture the Holy Sepulchre of the Lord seemed exciting and adventurous. Moreover, the Roman church promised complete remission of sin for those who died in battle with the infidels.
- A religious reform that fostered spirituality and religious zeal and opposed corruption in the church began in the middle of the tenth century at the monastery of Cluny, in Burgundy. The Cluniacs secured the papacy itself when Gregory VII took office in 1073.

It is traditional to number seven crusades, although only the first and the fourth had significant outcomes.

The First Crusade was set off by a volatile sermon preached by Pope Urban II at the Council of Clermont in 1095:

> O race of Franks . . . you are obligated to succour your brethren in the East, menaced by an accursed race, utterly alienated from God. The Holy Sepulchre of our Lord is polluted by the filthiness of an unclean nation. Recall the greatness of Charlemagne. O most valiant soldiers, descendants of invincible ancestors, be not degenerate. Let all hatred depart from among you, all quarrels stop, all wars cease. Start upon the road to the Holy Sepulchre to wrest that land from the wicked race and subject it to yourselves.[4]

The assembly shouted "Deus le veult" (God wills it) and became so excited that forty thousand persons left rather prematurely in August 1096 under Peter the Hermit and Walter the Penniless. Pillaging the countrysides and killing all the Jews they found, all but seven thousand of the crusaders were wiped out by Hungarians before they even reached Constantinople. The main army—possibly as large as three hundred thousand strong[5]—left in the fall of 1096 under Godfrey of Lorraine. Although suffering a severe loss of men, they succeeded in capturing Nicea in 1097, Antioch in June 1098, and finally Jerusalem itself in 1099. An eyewitness, Raymond of Agiles, wrote a horrifying account of the slaughter of every man, woman, and child in the city, when "men rode in blood up to their knees and the bridle reins."[6]

The Europeans established petty states at Antioch and at Edessa (in southeast Turkey, near the border with Syria) and, in 1099, the Latin Kingdom of Jerusalem, which lasted until it was defeated by Saladin in 1187. The Europeans lived in ghettos, leaving no lasting impact on the area except for their fortifications.

The Second Crusade (1147–1149) was prompted by the fall of Edessa (in southeast Turkey, near the border with Syria) to the Turks in 1144. Instigated by the preaching of the contentious medieval mystic Bernard of Clairvaux, seventy thousand knights departed for the region; one-tenth reached Damascus, where they were exterminated.

The loss of Jerusalem in 1187 prompted the Third Crusade (1189–1192). The three leading rulers of Europe participated: the Holy Roman emperor Frederick Barbarossa, the English king Richard the Lionheart, and the French king Philip. The emperor drowned in Asia Minor and Philip returned to France in a huff after a quarrel with Richard. Richard was able to maintain control of Acre and other parts of the coast but suffered a severe defeat at the hands of Saladin in battle at the Horns of Hattim near the Sea of Galilee.

The Fourth Crusade (1203–1204) was one of the sorriest episodes in all of church history. The westerners changed their plan to attack Palestine by way of Egypt and decided instead to attack Constantinople, which they captured in 1203. In 1204 they sacked the city and pillaged the churches, robbing them of relics, gold, precious statuary, and other priceless valuables. The damage was more severe than the city would experience when it fell to the Muslims in 1453. The Latin Kingdom of Constantinople lasted until 1261.

A curious and tragic episode was the so-called Children's Crusade of 1212, when a twelve-year-old shepherd, Stephen, gathered a group of children (legend has it that the number swelled to thirty thousand) intent on rescuing the holy places in Palestine. They reached Marseilles, expecting the sea to part so that they could travel to the Holy Land <u>unimpeded</u>. Instead, they became the victims of two slave-dealers, Hugo Ferreus and William Poreus, who loaded the children onto seven ships. Two were shipwrecked on San Pietro off the coast of Sardinia. The others reached North Africa, where the surviving children were sold into slavery. Another group from Germany, led by ten-year-old Nicholas of Cologne, passed across the Alps to reach Brindisi in Italy. They set sail, but were never heard from again.

The other crusades fell flat, and by the end of the thirteenth century Europe knew that the Crusades were over. The last European-held areas in the Middle East—Tyre, Sidon, Haifa, Beirut, and Acre—were retaken by the Muslims.

The unsettling effects and the permanent impact of the Crusades on Europe and on Christian-Muslim relations can scarcely be exaggerated. They created a more unified and hostile Islam, with which the Eastern church had to deal. They contributed to the depopulation of Europe, which was already underpopulated. They led to the increase in skepticism, the sale of indulgences, and the spread of heresies from the Balkans to the West (for example, the Bogomiles, who influenced the French Cathari or Albigenses). In addition, they introduced sexually transmitted diseases into Europe. Not least was the spectacle of the church—not simply the secular rulers—organizing armies and military campaigns, something previously unheard of and still completely repugnant to Eastern Christians. This set the precedent and helped to provide a rationale for the Western church to organize "crusades" against "infidels" (Christian "heretics") in its own midst, in Europe. The Western church made provisions for the Inquisition in the early 1200s, as we shall see below.

New military-monastic orders were founded in connection with the Crusades. The Templars were founded in 1118 and given a place near the temple site in Jerusalem. Taking vows of poverty, chastity, and obedience, they were the main bulwarks of defense of the Latin Kingdom of Jerusalem. They persisted after the end of the Crusades and were involved in a number of military campaigns and scandals. The Hospitalers or Knights of St. John were given the care of the sick at a hospital in Jerusalem that had been founded by Charlemagne. The Teutonic Knights were founded in Palestine in 1190 and later relocated in Germany, from where they pushed east to Prussia, engaging in missionary activities and nationalistic wars.

The Crusades nonetheless stimulated considerable intellectual ferment, resulting in the rediscovery of Aristotle and other classics (preserved also by the Spanish Muslims). It might not be pure coincidence that many of the great universities of Europe were founded in the Crusade period. In addition, the Crusades gave strong impetus to East-West trade and contributed to the decline of feudalism and the rise of national states.

Conclusion

The conquests of Islam caused Christendom the loss of approximately half of the territory in which it had become predominant, affecting more severely the Eastern church than the Western one. Although Muslims, Jews, and Christians would find coexistence possible in some areas (notably Spain and, for a considerable period, Lebanon), the tensions created by the Muslim conquests and the violent Christian response in the Crusades have obvious ongoing effects to the present day.

8

SCHOLASTICS, FRIARS, HERETICS, AND MYSTICS:
Crises of Spirituality

Lord, make me an instrument of your peace:
where there is hatred, let me sow love;
where there is injury, pardon;
where there is discord, unity;
where there is doubt, faith;
where there is error, truth;
where there is despair, hope;
where there is darkness, light.
O divine Master, grant that I may not so much seek
to be consoled, as to console;
to be understood, as to understand;
to be loved, as to love.
For it is in giving that we receive;
it is in pardoning that we are pardoned;
it is in dying that we are born to eternal life.

—attributed to Francis of Assisi[1]

The issue: How much diversity of spiritual practice could the church tolerate?

The period 1100–1500, the height of the Middle Ages, was not only the time of the Crusades and the Great Papal Schism but also of innovative forms of spirituality and theologizing in Europe. It was the time of scholasticism, mystics, new monastic movements, heretics, and calls for reform of the church. New movements often alarm the establishment, and each of these developments evoked a response.

Medieval Scholasticism

Scholasticism (from "school") refers to the kind of theologizing characteristic of the universities, cathedral schools, and monastic schools that emerged during this period. A common task of such theology was to assess the relationship of reason and faith, that is, of philosophy and theology, of the classical tradition and inherited Christian beliefs. How much of Christian truth can be known apart from divine revelation? Is "natural theology" possible?

The *method* of the scholastics was often dialectic: on each topic or question the opinions of past theologians would be arranged pro and con, after which a synthesis might be offered.[2] Thomas Aquinas adopted this method in his *Summas*. The *form* in which the scholastics speculated centered on the question of "universals" or Platonic "forms" or "ideas," that is, whether a universal concept exists apart from any individual representative of it. Does "the Good" exist prior to any concrete manifestation of goodness or the category of "tree" apart from any individual tree? What is the relation of language to reality? Absolute realists, like Anselm, held that universals exist *ante rem*, before and apart from the individual. Nominalists, like Abelard and most late scholastics, held that they are mere names for similar categories of individuals and exist *post rem*, after the individual. And moderate realists, like Thomas Aquinas, argued that universals exist only *in re*, in connection with individual objects.

Anselm, Abelard, and Peter Lombard represent the early period of scholasticism. Thomas Aquinas represents the middle period, and Duns Scotus and William of Occam the late period.

Anselm of Canterbury (1033–1109)

Anselm was profoundly convinced of the rationality of revealed truth. As he expressed it, "I believe in order that I may understand." He was a realist in the universals controversy and had a high estimate of the dialectical method. He is remembered for two contributions to Christian thought.

The first, the "ontological argument" for the existence of God, was based on the idea that human beings can conceive of a being than which nothing can be greater. Because existence is greater than nonexistence and necessity greater than contingency, such a being must necessarily exist or else anything that does in fact exist would be greater, which would contradict the conception. Anselm thus sought to prove God's existence from the structure of human thought itself.

The second, the "satisfaction theory" of the atonement, addressed the nature of Jesus' work. Christian theologians had never articulated a systematic explanation of precisely *how* the work of Jesus is effective for human salvation. Early Christians variously thought of Christ as teacher, as a victor over the power of the devil, as a ransom paid by God (sometimes to the devil) to gain control of humanity, as a sacrifice to God, or as a bestower of incorruption and immortality. Anselm found all such attempts inadequate and suggested instead a conception that fit the assumptions of honor and justice in feudal society. He viewed all of society as a grand hierarchy. Offenses committed against a superior are more serious than those committed against a peer or an inferior. God is the great overlord, of infinite power. Human sin is therefore infinite offense and requires infinite "satisfaction." How could a finite being offer infinite satisfaction? It was impossible—and therefore necessary that God become man.[3] Only the God-man could take our place and render satisfaction to God. But even the life of Jesus could not make such satisfaction, because Jesus owed a perfect life to God. His voluntary death, however, was more than required, and this produced an infinite reward (merit) that could be applied to others.

Peter Abelard (1079–1142)

A brilliant lecturer and thinker, Abelard attracted huge follow-ings with his lectures. By 1115 he was a canon of Notre Dame in Paris, when he began a romantic relationship and a secret marriage with Heloise, the niece of a fellow canon, Fulbert. After the enraged uncle had Abelard emasculated, he became a monk and she the head of a little nunnery east of Paris, the Paraclete. Abelard's autobiogra-phy, *The Story of My Misfortunes*,[4] and his correspondence with Heloise are fascinating historical documents.

Abelard rejected all prior atonement theories as unworthy of a good God. Satan has no just claims upon humanity, nor does God's anger need to be placated. The death of Jesus is not a cosmic event but a moral example of infinite divine love. "We love because he first loved us" (cf. 1 John 4:19).

Although somewhat doubtful about the possibilities of natural theology, Abelard believed that the Greeks had come close to the concept of the Trinity with their view of the Prime Mover, the Logos, and the world soul.

Peter Lombard (ca. 1100–1160)

Peter Lombard's copious compendium of quotations from the church fathers, councils, and creeds in his *Four Books of Sentences* was used by students even to the time of Martin Luther. He is remembered also as the first to distinguish between sacraments and sacramentals and to insist that there are seven sacraments (baptism, confirmation, penance, marriage, ordination, Eucharist, and last rites [extreme unction]).

Thomas Aquinas (1225–1274)

Thomas, who represents the high point of medieval scholasti-cism, was born into nobility at Aquino, halfway between Rome and Naples. He studied in Paris with the German Albertus Magnus (ca. 1193–1280), who was a moderate realist: "universals" exist *ante rem* in the mind of God, *in re* in the things themselves, and *post rem* in our understanding. Although Thomas was active in church affairs over a good part of Europe, his intellectual achievement met with opposition from those in the Augustinian tradition.

Among Thomas's voluminous writings are the two *Summas* (summaries of the faith), the *Summa contra Gentiles,* written on request by the Dominican order for aid in converting Muslims and Jews in Spain, and the *Summa Theologica,* for Christian readers. In both Thomas maintains that the aim of all theological investigation is to arrive at a knowledge of human origin and destiny. Human reason is highly useful in this endeavor, but it must be supplemented by the revelation in the Bible and interpreted in the light of the church fathers and councils. If not all Christian truths can be demonstrated by reason, none of them is contrary to reason.

A good half of the first *Summa* deals with matters that are accessible to human reason alone. Among these are the famous five "ways" (arguments) for the existence of God, most of them adapted from Aristotle:[5]

- *God as Prime Mover.* If we define motion as the change from potentiality to actuality, we cannot conceive that something is the cause of its own motion, and we must posit a Prime Mover, which is God.
- *God as first efficient cause.*[6] Nothing can be the efficient cause of itself, and the conception of an endless chain of causes is absurd. We must therefore posit a first efficient cause, which is God.
- *God as noncontingent (necessary) being.* Everything we experience can be conceived of as either existing or not existing, that is, as contingent. Contingent beings have the potential not to exist. Infinity can be defined as the actualizing of all contingencies, including the nonexistence of all things at the same time. But if at some point nothing existed, then nothing could come into being. There must therefore be at least one noncontingent (necessary) being, and that is God.
- *God as perfection.* The ability to say that something is more or less hot or cold or whatever the case may be presupposes the conception of the utmost, the perfect, the ultimate, which is God.

- *God as intelligent designer.* Even inanimate objects—heavenly bodies, for example—exhibit predictable behavior and act not fortuitously but from design and purpose. But whatever lacks intelligence cannot act purposefully unless directed by an intelligent being, which is God. (Only this of the five arguments posits a *personal* God.)

God for Thomas is first cause, pure actuality, the most real and perfect being, absolute substance, and the source and goal of all things.

Thomas includes much in the second half of the first *Summa* about the value of divine revelation, which guides one to the ultimate objective of human life—the beatific vision of God in eternity.

The *Summa Theologica*, addressed to Christians, is an attempt to expound and defend the whole body of Christian doctrine and dogma. It runs to twenty-one volumes, with thirty-eight full treatises in dialectical form. Of this mass of material two examples stand out.

First, on the relation of grace and merit, Thomas argues that human salvation is possible only through the free and unmerited grace of God, which restores fallen human nature and provides forgiveness of sins. This grace, however, is possible only because the death of Jesus Christ creates infinite super-merit. A human being who experiences grace is enabled to do good works. All Christians are obliged to follow the commands of the gospel, while the counsels of the gospel are binding only on monastics. God's grace, moreover, is channeled through the sacraments, of which there are seven instituted by Jesus (baptism, confirmation, Eucharist, penance, last rites, ordination, and marriage). Each of these has substance and form, understood in Aristotelian terms. In the greatest of the sacraments, the Eucharist, the substance of bread and wine—although not their "accidents," their appearance—actually changes into the true body and blood of Christ. This doctrine is known as transubstantiation (change of substance). The celebration of the Eucharist is therefore a repetition of the crucifixion in which the priest offers to God the body and blood of Christ.

Thomas asserts that, although God directly forgives the eternal punishment of sin for those who sincerely repent, temporal guilt and punishment remain, which are treated by the sacrament of penance. Penance is accomplished on Earth and in an extension of time, purgatory. A remission of all or part of the temporal punishment owing to sin is an "indulgence," which is the application to a person of the superfluous merit of someone else, whether the Virgin Mary or another saint. In the sacrament of penance, the church has jurisdiction over the removal of temporal punishment.

Second, Thomas distinguishes four kinds of law. Eternal law refers to the pure rationality of God and the universe as such. Natural law is ethical precepts that reflect eternal law, directing human beings to their earthly ends. These laws, imprinted on the human heart, can be known apart from revelation and therefore apply to all humanity, not only to Christians. Human laws, laws of specific human societies, should be derived from natural law, applying it to different contexts. Divine law, found in Scripture, directs human beings to their eternal end.

Thomas Aquinas was canonized in 1323 by Pope John XXII. In 1567 Pope Pius V proclaimed him Doctor of the Church (as part of the reaction to Protestantism), and on June 29, 1923, his authority as teacher was reiterated by Pope Pius XI, who required the study of Thomas by all students of philosophy and theology in the church.

Thomas was a Dominican, and his critics often came from a rival order, the Franciscans. Several Franciscans were English, including the following two exemplars.

Duns Scotus (ca. 1254–1308)

If Thomas found the central core of human nature in intellect and rationality, Duns Scotus[7] located it in will and love. According to Scotus, the doctrines of the church might not be against reason but they might be philosophically improbable. The source for the authority of church doctrine is not reason but rather the church.

William of Occam (Ockham) (ca. 1300–1349)

William, the last great scholastic, was a convinced nominalist and certain that we cannot derive valid concepts by abstraction. This approach promoted individualism, involved a divorce between philosphy and traditional theology, and therefore confronted human beings with a choice between abandoning church doctrine or accepting it on the basis of the authority of the church. William chose the latter. According to William, the church's authority is based on Scripture—not the papacy, especially when it lays claim to secular power. The church in essence is the community of believers, any one of which, including the pope, can fall into error.

Via Antiqua Versus Via Moderna

By the time of Martin Luther, scholasticism was spent. Theologians referred to Thomism and moderate realism as the "via antiqua" (the old way) and to nominalism as the "via moderna" (the new way). The dispute between the two can be found yet in the clash between Martin Luther, representing the via moderna, and his opponents, many of whom were Dominicans who represented the via antiqua.[8]

The Friars

From the eighth to the twelfth centuries almost all Western monks were Benedictines, including several spin-off movements such as that of Cluny and the Cistercians. As mentioned above, several "military" orders were founded during the Crusades—the Templars, Hospitalers, Teutonic Knights, and others. The thirteenth century saw the rise of several new monastic orders, the most important of which are known as friars (brothers), or mendicant (begging) orders, despite that fact that the founder of one such order called his followers to work for their living.

Friars differed from Benedictine monks in several ways. Monks lived an enclosed life; friars lived in the world. Monks often came from the upper classes and monasteries often became wealthy; friars—especially the Franciscans, who sought to follow the pattern of the humble life of Jesus and the first apostles—ministered to outcasts and the lowly. And friars were much more democratically organized than were Benedictines.

The main reason for the rise and success of the friars was undoubtedly the character of their founders, Francis of Assisi and Dominic de Guzman.

Francis of Assisi (1182–1226)

John Bernardone was nicknamed Francis ("the Frenchman") for his fondness for the French. The son of a rich merchant in Assisi, Italy, he underwent a sudden conversion while stricken with a serious illness. He then determined to find "perfection" and, following the words of Jesus in Matt 19:21, gave up all his possessions. He lived in prayer and poverty outside of town and gradually attracted a group of followers to lead the same life, going about the towns in the hill country, working at the harvests, and sleeping in the open or with lepers whom they nursed. They all took a vow of poverty, vowing never to own anything either as individuals or as a group. Francis taught that only those who themselves had stood barefoot in the marketplace, asking for alms, could have true compassion for the poor. They preached and cared for the sick and were known as the Lord's jesters because of their lightheartedness.

Francis had a curious devotion to nature and to animals. He once preached a sermon to his "little sisters the birds," and his "Canticle of the Sun" (which is related to his hymn "All Creatures of Our God") is the first poem composed in Italian.

In the year 1209 Francis and eleven of his companions went to Rome to ask Pope Innocent III to confirm their rule of absolute poverty and devotion to good works. After some hesitation, he did. They were to be known as *fratres minor* (little brothers), wear a dark gray habit, and go barefoot. Francis spent the rest of his life organizing groups that would form an order. In 1217 he divided his followers in Italy into friaries (provinces), and in 1223 he drew up an order for his friars and established friaries for women (minoresses).

Francis died in 1226, with the wounds of the crucified body of Jesus (stigmata) on his hands, feet, and side. After the amazingly short period of two years, he was canonized.

The Franciscans underwent divisions over the question of communal poverty. But the Order of Friars Minor (O.F.M.) continued to cultivate popular preaching and piety, fostering such practices as the adoration of the creche at Christmas, the stations of the cross, miracles, and the doctrine of the immaculate conception of Mary (the idea that she was conceived without original sin). Franciscans were concerned with missions to the Muslims, founding houses in Palestine and Egypt. They were the first to preach in central Africa, and some traveled through Persia, India, and Tibet to China, where they found Nestorian Christians living. Other missionaries went to Sumatra, Java, and Borneo. Several prominent scholars were Franciscans, among them William of Occam, Roger Bacon, and Nicholas of Lyra, who influenced the Reformers.

Dominic de Guzman (1170–1221)

Dominic de Guzman was the son of a Spanish nobleman who as a priest was sent to convert heretics in southern France (the Cathari). Concerned that the ignorance of the priests was part of the problem, he established a group in Toulouse that would foster the ongoing education of priests and organize efforts to counter the spread of heresy. The group called itself "preaching friars," and is known to this day as the Preaching Order (O.P., "Ordo Praedicatorum"). Dominic died in 1221 and was canonized in 1234.

The Dominicans wore a white habit with a black mantle. They spread out over Europe and Britain as missionaries, emphasizing learning and education, always countering ignorance and heresy, and establishing schools of theology. The Franciscans, in contrast, forbade books. In France the Dominicans came to be known as Jacobins, after their house in Paris, which was under the patronage of St. James [Jacques], whose name is derived from the Hebrew "Jacob."

The Dominicans trained many great scholars, among them Albertus Magnus and Thomas Aquinas. Because of their theological expertise, they often held leadership positions in the Inquisition. They are still today one of the most influential orders in the Roman Catholic Church.

Augustinians and Others

Other similar movements emerged at roughly the same time. The Augustinians, who followed the monastic rule attributed to the great church father and his disciples, were formed in Italy in the thirteenth century by groups of hermits. Their most famous friar was Martin Luther.

The Waldenses, a group of wandering lay preachers founded by Peter Waldo or Valdez (d. 1217) in France, would probably have become a Roman Catholic order if the pope had approved them (he did not). A kind of proto-Reformation movement, the Waldenses survived over the centuries and still exist in Italy.

Medieval Heresies and the Rise of the Inquisition

Groups unauthorized by the established church emerged in the West during the period of the Crusades, in some cases probably the result of the importing of dualistic ideas from the Balkans or the Levant. The Roman church responded to heresies, especially the Cathari, with the full-blown Inquisition.

The Cathari (Albigenses)

Between 1140 and 1160 a dualist heresy spread from northern Europe (Cologne and Liege) southward into France, penetrating into the French region of Languedoc and taking root also in northern Spain, northern Italy, and what is now Albania. The movement had different names in different places. Because it seems to have come into Western Europe from Bulgaria, followers of this movement were sometimes known as Bulgars ("bougres" in French, the source of the obscenity "bugger"). In Italy they were called Patarines. In France, they were commonly known as Albigenses, from their concentration in the area of Albi. They were also known by the term Cathari (from the Greek *katharos,* "pure"), which originated in northern Europe. The dualist beliefs of the Cathari had something in common with ancient Gnosticism and Manichaeism. In their *public* teaching the Cathari urged the literal interpretation of the New Testament. True Christians obeyed Jesus' commands that forbade oaths, lying, stealing, and killing, and required chastity and charity. The Bible was read in the vernacular. The Christian sacraments and ostentatious houses of worship were rejected.

The *esoteric* teaching to potential converts, however, was much more elaborate. This world is evil because its creator is the prince of darkness. To redeem lost souls the supreme God sent Jesus—but not in real human flesh. The redemption of the soul is possible only when one learns to pray in the name of Christ (especially by means of a mystical use of the Lord's Prayer) and by receiving the *consolamentum,* the closest thing in the movement to a sacrament (which involved the laying on of hands and placing the Gospel of John on the head of the candidate). Those who receive this rite become members of the "perfect"; potential full members are "believers," who would marry, hold property, and even conform outwardly to the Roman church. Without redemption, however, the soul remains a prisoner of the flesh and is condemned to an endless cycle of reincarnations. Sexual acts, which produce new bodies, are not divinely sanctioned; marriage is no better than prostitution. The perfect even abstained from eating the products of reproduction, such as milk, cheese, and eggs. Constant prayer and asceticism were encouraged; three days of the week were devoted to fasting on bread and water, and there were reports of the practice of "endura," suicide by fasting in order to avoid further contamination by the world.

Although exhibiting many varieties, the theology (or mythology) behind the teachings was generally one of two kinds. The absolute dualists—the main group in southern France after ca. 1170—taught the eternity of evil. Lucifer, son of the eternal principle of evil, invaded heaven and beguiled one-third of the angels to fall. Up to this time the angels had body, soul, and spirit. Lucifer seduced the souls of the angels, which he made to inhabit the bodies created on Earth by the devil. Moderate dualists variously taught that Lucifer was the son of the good God who rebelled in heaven and was cast out with his followers. Lucifer then made the world and placed in it the bodies of Adam and Eve. Most Cathari believed that Christ, Mary, and the Gospel writer John were all angelic beings.

The Inquisition stamped out this movement within one century.

Other Groups

Dissidents of various sorts can be found throughout the Middle Ages, and charges of heresy are even more common. Some scholastics were accused of heretical beliefs, as was Abelard by Bernard of Clairvaux. Muslim scholars of Aristotle in Spain, Averroës (d. 1198) for example, influenced several scholastics. In addition, mystics such as Meister Eckhart were accused of pantheism.

More pathological manifestations were groups such as the Adamists, who worshiped in the nude, and various flagellants, who marched through towns in single file, flogging the person in line ahead and proclaiming full salvation to all who persevered in flagellation for thirty-three days. Witchcraft and sorcery, much of which was caused by sociological factors—gender inequality, for example— were considered heresy by the Inquisition (Roger Bacon was unique in viewing witchcraft as a fraud or a delusion).

The Inquisition

Although for centuries local bishops had made "inquiries" into the beliefs of their flocks, the church—once the object of persecution itself—had agreed with the church father John Chrysostom (ca. 347–407) that "to put a heretic to death would be a crime that cannot be expiated."[9] Although Christian secular rulers such as Justinian and Charlemagne might use the sword to advance the faith, the idea that *the church* would not only sanction but also use the death penalty would have struck church leaders as a grotesque obscenity. But a kind of precedent was established when the church organized crusades against the Muslims. It was perhaps not a long step from that to actions against "nonbelievers" and dissidents in its own territories.

The earliest known case of the execution of Cathari in Europe was the burning by King Robert of France of thirteen Cathari in 1022 (the *church* had not yet carried out executions). Mob violence soon led to the burning of Cathari in other places as well.

To prevent and contain heresy, ca. 1215, Pope Innocent III began the practice of sending out papal missionaries, sometimes accompanied by armies, as inquisitors. But the full-blown Inquisition was

organized by Pope Gregory IX ca. 1229. It was to have two parts:
(1) The general inquisition, in which the papal inquisitor would
solemnly charge all inhabitants of a village to accuse all whom they
suspected. In addition, spies were hired and clergy called on for this
task. Those who voluntarily surrendered were given penance. (2) The
special inquisition, in which the accused were questioned about their
beliefs and asked to name their friends. To be accused was de facto
to be considered guilty, and it was practically impossible to prove
one's innocence. No one who was accused would get off scot-free.

Not much more than a century later, the Cathari had been
expunged from Western Europe. The most notorious use of the
Inquisition, however, that in Spain under Ferdinand and Isabel, was
to come later, as we will see.

Medival Piety: The Mystics

Almost no one in the Middle Ages doubted that this life is but a
preparation for the next. This belief gave meaning to life for everyone from pope to serf, and it made the church central. Human salvation was God's chief business, and the chosen instrument for
salvation was the church.

Scholars held to the ancient Ptolemaic worldview: the round
earth was surrounded by twelve concentric, transparent spheres in
which moved the planets, sun, moon, and stars. Beyond the universe was heaven, the abode of God and the saints. Common people, however, considered the earth flat, with Jerusalem at its center
Jerusalem. Somewhere to the east was the Garden of Eden. Hell
was beneath the earth—sometimes the stench came up through
clefts in the rocks—and the heavens revolved above the earth, par-
allel to it.

The worldview of the common person was given classic expression in the *Divine Comedy*, which was written by Dante Alighieri
(1265–1321) in Italian toward the end of his life. In this great poem
Dante's soul journeys to the pits of hell, witnessing the torments of
the damned. He is then led through the seven terraces of purgatory,
where the souls are purified. Finally he is led through the nine

heavens, the abode of the saints and angels in hierarchy. At the top is the Empyrean, the abode of God, where Dante's guide becomes St. Bernard. Bernard introduces Dante to the Virgin Mary, who finally assists Dante to the ultimate goal of medieval piety—the beatific vision of God, the goal shared by pope, peasant, and prince.

The piety of the Middle Ages expressed itself in a variety of mystics. Mysticism by its nature is almost impossible to define. Not a system of thought, it is more an attitude toward life and reality that assumes that underneath all diversity there is a unity, a central reality. Outward things are but shadows of this reality, and the goal of the mystic is to achieve union with the ultimate, that is, with God. What usually is sought is not merely peace with God but unity with God, complete fusion, so that the distinction between Creator and creature is overcome. A number of mystics and mystical movements indicate the variety of medieval mysticism.

Bernard of Clairvaux (1090–1153)

Bernard was a monk of the Cistercian order active in the reform of the papal curia and ever on the alert to charge his opponents with heresy. Well versed in the Bible, he preached eighty-six sermons just on the first chapter of the Song of Solomon, interpreting the text as an allegory of the love of the soul for Jesus. According to Bernard, there are three stages in the mystical experience: (1) consideration, believing the doctrines of the church; (2) contemplation, reflecting on the love of God in Jesus, producing the desire to imitate Christ; and (3) ecstasy, going outside of oneself into *raptus* (rapture), dropping into divinity as a drop of water falls into a glass of water—the substance remains, but the drop is absorbed and disolved into the all-embracing divine form.

Hildegard of Bingen (1098–1179)

Hildegard of Bingen was born to a noble family and with connections to high church and state officials. During most of her eighty-one years, she experienced pictorial visions along with interpretations in Latin. These visions would be written down and accompanied by paintings by women in her monastery.[10] Her final writing, *The Book of Divine Works,*[11] presents a grand sweep of salvation history from pre-creation to the final consummation. In it Hildegard is concerned to demonstrate the complementarity of the human genders as part of God's intention for the harmony of the universe. Hildegard's mystical theology gained the approval of Bernard and Pope Eugenius III.

Joachim of Fiore (Flora) (1132–1202)

Joachim represents a kind of sociological mysticism. He found three grand epochs in world history: (1) The age of the Father, which ran from Adam to Christ, was the time of slavery, works, marriage, and feudalism. (2) The age of the Son, which began with Christ, and would end, according to Joachim, in the year 1260. This was the age of the church, grace, clergy, and sacraments. (3) The age of the Spirit would begin soon, a golden age of contemplation and monasticism in which poverty and love would replace the wealth and arrogance of the church. This schema presupposes the relativity of truth in which the church itself would ultimately become irrelevant—a radical thought in the Middle Ages.

Meister Eckhart (1260–1327)

The best known of the German mystics, Eckhart lectured on philosophy at the University of Paris. Toward the end of his life he was tried for the heresy of pantheism (the idea that God and the universe are identical)—in spite of the fact that he thought he was espousing the practical side of the theology of his fellow Dominican Thomas Aquinas. The difficulty of interpreting Eckhart's sermons and essays centers on his attempt to express the inexpressible. His approach, however, includes the idea that God is Being itself in a state of flux, as symbolized in the doctrine of the Trinity. All creatures derive being from God; they have no true reality apart from God. The point of contact between humans and God is the "inner spark" of the soul: "God must be born in the soul." Christ is the pattern and example of this experience, which is superior to any outward rites of the church.

The Brethren of the Common Life

A non-monastic community founded in the fourteenth-century Netherlands, the Brethren of the Common Life produced the best-loved devotional tract of all time, *The Imitation of Christ* (ca. 1425), often attributed to Thomas à Kempis (1380–1471). It is organized into four "books": (1) Counsels on the Spiritual Life, (2) Counsels on the Inner Life, (3) On Inward Consolation, and (4) On the Blessed Sacrament (the Eucharist). Here is a sample:

> Firstly, be peaceful yourself, and you will be able to bring peace to others. A peaceful person does more good than a very learned man. A passionate person turns even good into evil, and readily listens to evil; but a good and peaceable person turns all things to good. The one who is truly at peace thinks evil of no one; but the one who is discontented and restless is tormented by suspicions beyond number.
>
> There are some who remain at peace with themselves and also with others. And some neither have peace in themselves nor allow others to have peace. . . . And there are some who are at peace with themselves, and who try to guide others into peace. But all our peace in this present life should depend on humble forbearance rather than on absence of adversity. He who knows the secret of endurance will enjoy the greatest peace. Such a one is conqueror of self, master of the world, a friend of Christ, and an heir of Heaven.[12]

Members of this group influenced some of the Reformers. One of them, Hieronymous Bosch (d. 1516), was one of the greatest painters of the time, known espeically for his *Garden of Earthly Delights,* although may others of his works are exceptionally done.

St. John of the Cross (1542–1591)

This Spaniard, a friend of St. Teresa, wrote several mystical works, among them *The Dark Night of the Soul.* Although he had at one time been imprisoned by the Inquisition, he was canonized in 1726 and made a Doctor of the Church in 1926.

Conclusion

The Middle Ages were scarcely the dull, static epoch many moderns think. Christian theology came to full maturity, and the authority of the church with its hierarchical structure, its canon law, and especially its assurance of future salvation provided a firm orientation to life in an age that was often dangerous. It was a time when the church resorted to force and violence to coerce conformity in its own midst. But it was also a time of intellectual ferment and creative theology, of an array of experiments in piety and belief, and of crisis and conflict that led inexorably to the modern period. The pluralism of Western religious piety in the twenty-first century has numerous parallels with that of medieval Europe.

9

THE REFORMATION
The Crisis of Salvation Once Again

Faith is a living and unshakeable conviction, a belief in the grace of God so assured that a person would die a thousand deaths for its sake. This kind of confidence in God's grace, this sort of knowledge of it, makes us joyful, high-spirited, and eager in our relations with God and with all humankind. That is what the Holy Spirit effects through faith. Hence, the person of faith, without being driven, willingly and gladly seeks to do good to everyone, serve everyone, suffer all kinds of hardships, for the sake of the love and glory of the God who has shown such grace. It is impossible, indeed, to separate works from faith, just as it is impossible to separate heat and light from fire.

—Martin Luther, "Preface to Romans"[1]

The issue: What is the relation between human activity and divine grace in Christian salvation, and what role do church structures have in it?

Perhaps the greatest crisis of Western Christianity in the second millennium was the complex of events known as the Reformation, which was begun by Martin Luther in the early sixteenth century. It permanently shattered the unity of Western Christendom as it stimulated creative theology and forms of spirituality.

Amazingly little has been written about the perceived need for reform in the church around 1500. Was there a general feeling that the church was in need of correction at all? To be sure, some writers were saying that the church, the "ark of salvation," had become a "ship of fools."[2] Moreover, the Avignon papacy and the Great Papal Schism had let loose nationalistic feelings (why should the English submit to a French papacy and pay taxes for its support?). Scholasticism was in decline, and the Inquisition had left a bad taste in parts of the West. There is some evidence also that morality was in decline. Clerical concubinage was widely practiced, and the church levied taxes on children of priests. Many bishops did not reside in the dioceses for which they were installed, and some held more than one office, in different areas (pluralism). Many clergy were ignorant, and superstition among the common people was rampant. It is nonetheless unclear whether things were worse in Europe in 1500 than at other times and places in church history.

Types of Reform

Prior to Martin Luther there were three kinds of attempts to reform and renew the church in Europe: doctrinal-nationalistic reform like that of John Wycliffe and John Huss, coercive orthodoxy like that of Ferdinand and Isabel in Spain, and humanistic reform like that advocated by Erasmus.

Doctrinal-Nationalistic Reform

John Wycliffe (1324–1384) studied at Oxford and was influenced by Augustine's ideas of grace and predestination. Wycliffe's conception of the church was feudal: God is the great overlord who gives the *use,* but not the *ownership,* of all positions, civil and ecclesiastical, to individuals. If the user abuses his trust, he forfeits his tenure. The import of such ideas for the papacy when the popes were located at Avignon (1309–1378) is obvious.

For Wycliffe, the Scriptures were the only law of the church (there is no canon law as such). Wycliffe therefore undertook the translation of the Bible from the Latin (the Vulgate) into English, the basis of all subsequent translations into our own day.

Wycliffe's most radical idea, however, was his attack on the doctrine of transubstantiation—that the priest's act in the Eucharist accomplishes the change of bread and wine into the substance of the body and blood of Christ. Wycliffe taught that the true body and blood are present along with the bread and wine, a view sometimes called consubstantiation. This attack cost him many followers and led to much opposition, even though, because of his popularity and powerful friends, he died in his bed.

As the Waldenses had done before him, Wycliffe sent out followers two-by-two to preach. These preachers came to be known as Lollards (the origin of the term is uncertain). But Wycliffe left no successor in England, and his influence continued instead in Prague in the movement of John (Jan) Huss, who had become acquainted with Wycliffe's ideas in a roundabout fashion.

In the mid-thirteenth century, the church in Bohemia became independent of the bishop of Mainz. When the Bohemian princess Anna married King Richard II of England, Bohemian students went to Oxford and brought back Wycliffe's ideas and writings, especially to the new university of Prague. John Huss (ca. 1370–1415) studied at Prague (Th.D., 1394) and was ordained a priest in 1401 while teaching at the university. Although agreeing with many of Wycliffe's doctrines, including predestination and the authority of the Bible, Huss was more conservative, not denying transubstantiation. But he was caught up in the attempts to overcome the Great Papal Schism by the imposition of unity and uniformity. Excommunicated in 1410, he then wrote his major work, *On the Church*.

In 1415 Huss was summoned to the Council of Constance and promised safe conduct by the emperor. There he was attacked by his enemies and imprisoned. On May 4, 1415, the council condemned John Wycliffe and ordered his long-buried body to be burned. Then, on July 6, 1415, the council condemned John Huss and burned him at the stake. He endured death with great courage. John Huss's death led to revolution in Bohemia, and many Hussites later joined the Reformation.

Wycliffe and Huss were forerunners of the Protestant Reformation in the sense that they protested against some of the same things and held to the sole authority of the Bible. But their conception of the gospel was closer to that of the medieval church than to the emphasis on radical grace on the part of the Reformers.

Coercive Orthodoxy

The changes that took place on the Iberian Peninsula during the fifteenth century were astounding. Long divided among Muslims, Jews, and Christians, the peninsula in 1400 contained six countries: Navarre, Aragon, Castile, Leon, Granada, and Portugal. In 1500 there were two: Spain and Portugal. This change was the result of the marriage in 1469 of Ferdinand, who inherited the rule of Aragon, and his cousin Isabel of Castile and Leon. In 1492 they conquered Granada, the last Muslim area on the peninsula; sent Columbus on his first voyage in which he "discovered" the New World; and forcibly required all Jews to convert to Christianity or leave their domains. (Estimates are that approximately 50,000 converted and approximately 165,000 were expelled.) Ten years later they gave the Moors (Muslims) the same choice.

Ferdinand and Isabel used the Spanish Inquisition to accomplish religious uniformity in line with the Roman church. The most notorious inquisitor was Torquemada, the grand inquisitor from 1483 to 1498. By his efforts in seeking out heretics and secret Jews or Moors, some ten thousand persons were burned in "acts of faith" (*autos de fe*). At the same time, Isabel made serious efforts at religious reform by education. To this end she appointed such able persons as Ximénez (1436–1517), the cardinal archbishop of Toledo.

When Ferdinand died in 1516 he passed control of all Spain to his grandson, Charles, who was also, as Charles V, elected Holy Roman Emperor.

Humanistic Reform

The revival of ancient Greek and Roman culture in Europe that we know as the Renaissance began in Italy when Petrarch (1304–1374) promoted ancient Latin classics by writers such as Cicero. Soon Greek and Latin classics were being translated into the modern languages, and the slogan "Back to the sources!" (namely, of Western culture) was heard. The classics were to be used as a critique of church society. For the Reformers, the slogan would mean back to the Bible, the source of Christianity. Along with this change of emphasis from scholasticism to the classics went a change from an emphasis on the next world to this, from God to humanity, and from saintly beauty to earthly beauty. The rediscovery of classic Greek art was taken up by a host of geniuses in painting, sculpture, and architecture, among them Leonardo da Vinci, Raphael, and Michelangelo. The period from Petrarch to Luther also witnessed the beginning of the scientific method (for example, see the section on Copernicus in chapter 11), geographical exploration (Diaz, da Gama, Columbus, Cabral, and others), improvements in the manufacture of paper, and the invention of the movable type ca. 1450 by Johann Gutenberg. The popes of the time generally served as patrons of the new styles in art.

The Renaissance in northern Europe took on a more generally humanistic aspect, with a stronger appeal for church reform. Typical of the movement is Erasmus of Rotterdam (1469–1536), a product of monastic schools who was influenced by the Brethren of the Common Life. Erasmus was ordained a priest in 1492 and then studied in Paris, where he became contemptuous of scholasticism. He prepared new editions of the classics and wrote several famous works, including *Manual of Christian Ethics, Education of a Christian Prince,* and satires such as *The Praise of Folly* and *Julius Excluded from Heaven.* Convinced that a purified biblical text would lead to the purification of Christian life, he translated the Bible and, in 1516, published one of the first critical editions of the Greek text of the New Testament.

Erasmus was a professor of theology in France when the Lutheran Reformation began. Although Erasmus and Luther shared criticisms of the Roman church and an emphasis on biblical authority, the former could not wholeheartedly support the latter's reform. Erasmus emphasized human reason and morality and the ambiguity of historical movements. He disliked personal controversy and died a Roman Catholic, although nine years after his death the Council of Trent declared him a heretic. The difference between Erasmus and Luther came to a head in their dispute over free will and predestination.[3]

Martin Luther (1483–1546)

The first of the Protestant Reformers, and the one who influenced all others was an Augustinian monk struggling with severe spiritual anxiety (he called this *Anfechtung*) to please the righteous and holy God. Martin Luther—came from Saxony and was encouraged by his father to become a lawyer—or at least marry a rich woman. He nonetheless quit law studies at Erfurt after narrowly escaping death from a bolt of lightning, when he purportedly cried out, "St. Anne, save me, and I shall become a monk."[4] On July 17, 1505, he entered the Augustinian monastery at Erfurt and threw himself into a grueling schedule of study and monastic discipline, taking his monastic vows in September 1506. His confessions sometimes lasted six hours, but his introspection and rigors only deepened his despair over pleasing God. He was ordained a priest in 1507 and celebrated his first Eucharist on May 2, later writing that he was then "terror-stricken" by offering something to the "living, eternal, and true God." His mentor, Johann von Staupitz, general of the Augustinians, ordered him to study at Wittenberg for his doctorate in Holy Scripture and to preach, thinking that Luther's struggles might thereby find some resolution. Luther was awarded the degree of Doctor of Theology on October 18, 1512 and began to lecture on the Psalms and Paul's letters.

The "Tower Experience" and the Ninety-five Theses

At some point between 1512 and 1517, the study of Psalms and Romans finally led to Luther's life-changing "tower experience"—the insight that God *bestows by grace* the righteousness (or justice) that God demands of sinful humans. God's justice is not demand but gift. This insight led to a new view of God as not only judge but especially deliverer, of the Scriptures as consisting of law and gospel, and of the church as the people of God, the "priesthood of all believers." It was for Luther liberating and exhilarating: "I felt exactly as if I had been born again, and I believed that I had entered paradise through widely open doors. . . ."

Luther's professorial activities helped the reputation of the University of Wittenberg, and, when he began his lifelong work as preacher in the city church, his calls for church reform began to have an effect. When he heard that the Dominican Johann Tetzel, who was hawking indulgences to finance the rebuilding of St. Peter's in Rome, had said that he was authorized to sell plenary indulgences to free departed souls in purgatory, Luther took offense.[5] On October 31, 1517, hoping to stimulate a debate on the matter, he posted on or at the door of the castle church in Wittenberg ninety-five theses with the title *Disputation on the Power and Efficacy of Indulgences*. The main point of the theses is that the church has no jurisdiction over the souls in purgatory. In addition, Luther insisted, works of penance should be undertaken willingly as an expression of living faith. Moreover, if the pope has authority to free souls from purgatory, he should do so without charge. The Ninety-five Theses are therefore part of an intramural discussion that turned out to be the beginning of a schism only because of the church's response. Originally written in Latin, the theses were soon translated into German and were widely distributed.

The Response to the Ninety-five Theses as the Beginning of the Protestant Reformation

It is no exaggeration to say that the response to Luther's Ninety-five Theses by the monasteries, the papacy, and the emperor created the Protestant Reformation. Johann Tetzel and Luther's archbishop, Albert, immediately reported Luther to Rome, where the pope suggested that this was a monastic dispute. Johannes von Eck, a Dominican professor at Ingolstadt, however, called Luther a Bohemian, suggesting that he was a Hussite. Luther was called to explain his views before the council of the Augustinians at Heidelberg, for which he composed his *Heidelberg Disputations,* a classical expression of Luther's "theology of the cross."

On August 7, 1518, the Dominicans succeeded in inducing Pope Leo X to demand Luther's appearance within sixty days on suspicion of heresy. Fearing death, Luther appealed for help to the elector Frederick the Wise to arrange for a hearing on German soil. Luther therefore met the papal legate Cardinal Cajetan at Augsburg on October 12–14. Cajetan was not authorized to make concessions and treated the matter as disciplinary; Luther wanted to discuss indulgences and the concept of the church's "treasury of merit." There was an impasse. On the way home, Luther first saw a copy of a letter in which the pope declared him a notorious heretic. In November, fearing excommunication, Luther called for a general church council to discuss the matter.[6]

On January 12, 1519, the emperor Maximilian I died. Among the possible successors were Charles I of Spain, Francis I of France, and Henry VIII of England. In one of the curious details of the Reformation, the pope supported Frederick the Wise, Luther's protector. In the end Charles (1500–1558) was unanimously elected on June 28, 1519 as Charles V—at the age of nineteen.

At the Leipzig debates of June 27–July 16, 1519, the main issue rapidly became that of authority in the church. Johannes von Eck used the Pseudo-Isidorean Decretals, mentioned in chapter 6, to support the claims of the papacy. Luther asserted that the pope rules by human—not divine—right and that Scripture was the ultimate authority in all matters of religion. Eck again called Luther a Bohemian and classified him with John Wycliffe and John Huss. Luther then came increasingly to speak of biblical authority—*sola scriptura,* the "formal principle of the Reformation."

In the spring of 1520, Leo X appointed another commission—this one including Eck and Cajetan—to examine Luther's doctrines. They drew up a bull that condemned forty-one errors ascribed to Luther. The pope signed the bull on June 15, 1520. It is known by its opening words, *Exsurge domine,* from the Latin of Ps 74:22: "Arise, O Lord, plead your cause; a wild boar has invaded your vineyard. . . ." When he heard about the bull Luther became belligerent and for the first time called the pope the antichrist of the book of Revelation. On December 10, 1520, students and professors of the University of Wittenberg gathered outside the eastern city gate at the city dump. A large bonfire was started. Luther threw into it a number of books that supported the papacy and then—probably on impulse—he threw in a copy of the papal bull. The die was cast.

Also in 1520, Luther wrote three memorable treatises. In "Address to the Christian Nobility of the German Nation" he demands that the German rulers take steps to reform the papacy and the whole church. "The Babylonian Captivity of the Church," written for theologians, deals with the sacraments, of which there are two, baptism and the Eucharist (or possibly three, including penance). And in "The Freedom of the Christian" Luther articulates his view of the relation between faith and good works and suggests that the Christian is "at the same time sinful and justified" (*simil justus et peccator*).

The emperor was not about to take Luther's advice in the first of these treatises. He banned Luther's books in the Netherlands. Frederick the Wise urged that Luther be given a hearing at the emperor's first diet, to be held at Worms in 1521. Just before the diet began, the pope issued another bull, *Decet romanum pontificem* (It is fitting that the Roman pontif . . .), which formally excommunicated Luther. Luther appeared before the emperor Charles V on April 17–18, 1519. He was asked whether he was the author of a number of books placed on a table in front of him and whether he would recant any part of them. He answered the first question in the affirmative but asked for time to consider the second. He was given twenty-four hours. The next day, in a larger auditorium, he said it was impossible to give a simple answer, because the books were of different kinds. Some were books of edification, which no one could reject. Some dealt with papal abuse, the denial of which would occasion guilt. And some were written against individuals in defense of the gospel; if he had been in error or too harsh in any of these he would recant. The emperor demanded a clear answer whether or not Luther would retract the errors in his books. Luther's reply is classic: "Unless I am convicted by Scripture and plain reason . . . my conscience is captive to the Word of God. I cannot and I will not recant anything, for to go against conscience is neither right nor safe. Here I stand, I cannot do otherwise. God help me. Amen."[7] Fearing for his life, Luther left Worms on April 16 and was "kidnapped" by his friends and taken to the Wartburg Castle, where he resided from May 15, 1521, to March 1522.

The Edict of Worms was issued on May 15, 1521. The emperor placed Luther under his ban, making him an outlaw. Luther's teachings were proscribed, and the first Lutheran martyrs were killed in Brussels in 1523. The Protestant break with Rome was formal and final.

THE SETTLEMENT OF THE RELIGIOUS QUESTION

1521 The Diet of Worms: Lutheranism was proscribed and Luther declared an outlaw.

1526 The Diet of Speyer: With the absence of the emperor and the Turks a common menace, the princes adopted a new principle: *cujus regio, ejus religio*—"whose is the reign, his the religion," which means that the religion of a territory would be that of its prince or secular ruler. Lutheranism would be tolerated in areas ruled by Lutherans. This principle would eventually be adopted at the Peace of Augsburg.

1529 The Diet of Speyer: Charles demanded the nullification of the decisions of the 1526 Diet of Speyer. Lutherans objected and were called "the protesting estates"—the origin of the term Protestant.

1530 The Diet of Augsburg: Lutherans presented to the emperor a classic summary of their teachings, the *Augsburg Confession*, written by Luther's right-hand man, Philipp Melanchthon. This diet reaffirmed the decision of the Diet of Worms.

1547 War between Lutherans (the Schmalkald League) and Catholics broke out. Lutheranism seemed crushed.

1548 The Augsburg Interim: Charles V granted a few concessions to Protestants, including marriage of clergy. The Leipzig Interim allowed additional privileges to Lutherans in Saxony.

1555   The Peace of Augsburg. In the absence of the emperor, with little influence from the pope, and after intensive negotiations, the princes agreed that there would be equal rights in the empire for Roman Catholics and Lutherans. The pattern existing since the time of the emperor Constantine had been broken. Each prince would determine which one of the two should be tolerated in his territory. Church lands seized by Lutherans prior to 1552 were to be retained by them. Freedom of migration was provided. But the failure to grant tolerance to other Protestants resulted in the Thirty Years War of the next century.

1648   The Peace of Westphalia ended the Thirty Years War and provided for the recognition of Calvinists.

1689   The Toleration Act in England after the Puritan revolution provided religious toleration alongside Anglican establishment—except for Roman Catholics and Unitarians.

1789   The Constitution of the United States—for the first time in Christian history—provided for the disestablishment of religion and complete religious freedom—not merely toleration.[8]

Luther Consolidates the Movement

Luther's reflections during his stay at the Wartburg Castle led him to conclude that the Christian has the right to confess sins directly to God alone; the priest has no special authority to pronounce sins forgiven. He also came to the conviction that the Eucharist is not a sacrifice offered by the priest to God; the faithful recipient receives the true body and blood of Christ in, with, and under the bread and wine. Most surprising in some respects, this monk came to assert that monastic vows are not binding: the vow of chastity is contrary to human nature ("it is not possible to remain chaste without marriage"), the vow of poverty was mostly a sham, and true obedience belongs solely to God.

Luther's activities at Wartburg centered on his translation of the Bible into the official German of Saxony—the first German translation from the original languages instead of the Latin (the Vulgate version). He accomplished this task in the incredibly short span of eleven weeks. It was published in September 1522.

It grated on Luther that the course of the Reformation in Wittenberg was now in the hands of others. Reports came to him that "enthusiasts"—fanatics who claimed direct inspiration from the Holy Spirit—such as Andreas Carlstadt and the "three prophets of Zwickau" were gaining influence there, smashing church statues and windows, forbidding infant baptism, and proclaiming that the old order was now abolished.[9] This was too much. Luther returned to Wittenberg on March 6, 1522 and forbade the use of force and the neglect of Christian freedom. What is not forbidden in Scripture— good music, art, marriage of clergy, fasting, images—should be permitted. Lutherans therefore retained the structure of the liturgy of the mass and proved their movement to be a relatively conservative reformation. What matters is the gospel of justification by grace through faith alone.

If Luther's liturgical conservatism is evident in his opposition to the enthusiasts, his political conservatism had unfortunate results in the Peasants' War of 1524–1526. Already from the time of the Diet of Worms Luther had warned his supporters against using force to deal with dissidents and heretics. He opposed all who took up arms to bring about religious or social change. For decades the peasants of Germany had complained about inflation, taxes, and the oppression of the princes and landowners. They had organized the Bundschuh League in 1493 and gradually began to incorporate religious ideas into their movement. When Luther spoke about the freedom of a Christian, the equality of all before God, avarice of the merchants, and greed among the clergy, they naturally heard these as not only religious but also political statements. When the Countess of Lüpfen in the southwest Black Forest in June 1524 demanded that the peasants gather strawberries and snailshells for a banquet, it was simply the last straw. One thousand peasants revolted, and the violence broke out throughout one-third of Germany and Austria. The peasants set forth their generally reasonable demands in February 1525 in twelve articles: each community should have the right to choose its own pastor, serfdom should be abolished, forced labor regulated, rents be justly fixed, and seizure of land without fair payment abolished.

The movement, however, went out of control. In Saxony and Thuringia, Thomas Münzer (1490–1525), a well-educated theologian who had turned enthusiast, preached a sermon calling on the elector of Saxony to use force to establish an apocalyptic kingdom on Earth by mercilessly spilling the blood of the godless. Dozens of monasteries and castles were destroyed in the war. But the princes defeated Münzer, who was beheaded, and they became more ruthless in suppressing the peasants.

In May 1525 Luther wrote the infamous treatise "Against the Murderous Thieving Hordes of Peasants," exorting the princes to suppress the revolt with negotiations. If talking failed, they should use their God-given swords to punish the rebels severely. The tactless language of this treatise repelled many even who supported Luther's movement.

In the middle of the violence, Luther created another institution that has given the church a great many leaders and theologians: the parsonage. On June 13, 1525, at the age of forty-one, Luther married Katherine von Bora, a nun. They celebrated with a dance at the town hall. He did it, he said, to spite the pope and to give witness to his faith before his approaching martyrdom. Luther's family gave him much joy.

In Luther's later life there appeared another infamous treatise, one that reflects a reversal of his earlier opinion. In 1523 he had written *That Jesus Christ Was Born a Jew,* in which he argued that Jews should be dealt with in a humanitarian way. In 1543, however, just three years before his death, he wrote *On the Jews and Their Lies*.[10] Disappointed and outraged that the Jews had not converted to Christianity after his purification of it, Luther lists the "false boasts" of the Jews, their supposed erroneous interpretation of "messianic" texts of the Old Testament, and their "calumnies" against Jesus and Mary. In the notorious final section, Luther suggests that the Jews should be persecuted and reduced to agrarian servitude. If trouble persists, they should be expelled from the country. That this document played an important role in later anti-Semitic actions in Germany is certain, although the degree to which this is the case is disputed.

Lutheranism, a name that Luther repudiated,[11] retained from Luther its "material principle," justification by grace through faith, and its "formal principle," Scripture alone. Related to these are the emphases on the theology of the cross, the proper distinction between law and gospel, and the distinction between God's "left-hand" work in the secular realm and "right-hand" activity, the justification of human beings (this latter concept is usually known as the doctrine of the two kingdoms).

Ulrich (Huldreich) Zwingli (1484–1531)

The first major Swiss Refomer was Ulrich Zwingli. Influenced during his studies by Erasmus, he was ordained a priest in 1506, when he became parish pastor at Glarus. He moved to Zurich in 1519, where he remained until his death. There he became acquainted with Luther's writings, although he would not readily admit influence from Luther. In his sermons he attacked the doctrines of purgatory, prayer to the saints, and monasticism, as well as the authority of the papacy.

Zwingli's reform in Zurich took place between 1522 and 1525. During that time priests and nuns married, fees for baptism and marriage were abolished, statues and images were removed from the churches, and, during Holy Week in 1525, the mass was abolished. Zwingli himself married on April 2, 1524. One of Zwingli's most radical tenets was the rejection of any doctrine of the bodily presence of Christ in the Eucharist; he articulated instead a symbolic interpretation of the "words of institution" ("this is my body . . . blood"). But his emphasis on the authority of the Christian community through the organs of civil government was reminiscent of the medieval pattern of Catholic theocracy, except that Zwingli emphasized that the elect, who can be identified by their good works, constitute the community, so that the church and the state are composed of the same individuals.

Zwingli's reform was considerably more humanistic and radical than was Luther's. Unlike Luther, who relied on God's grace through depressions and elations, faith for Zwingli was something like psychological health and stability. A startling contrast was Zwingli's view of law. Luther taught that God's law—there is no natural law binding on Christians—produces resistance in the human heart, incites sin, and thereby drives a person in despair to total reliance on God's grace. For Zwingli the gospel itself is a "new law" that serves as the basis of civil law, an idea Luther found abominable.

The conflict between Zwingli and Luther came to a head at the Marburg Colloquy of 1529. Philip of Hesse, Luther's strongest military defender, feared attack by the emperor's troops and wanted to form a league of all German and Swiss Protestants. Discussions took place at Marburg to determine whether there was sufficient doctrinal agreement to accomplish this. In the end the two sides agreed on fourteen of fifteen articles. But because of Luther's insistence on the real presence of Christ in the Eucharist, they reached an impasse, and a union or federation was to be impossible.[12]

John Calvin and Reformed Protestantism

Calvinism, known as Reformed Protestantism in distinction from Lutheranism, came to be the most international form of the movement. Rejecting the territorial principle, Calvinism became the dominant form of Protestantism in Switzerland, France, the Netherlands, England, Scotland, New England, Lithuania, Poland, and Hungary.

John Calvin (1509–1564) studied for the priesthood in Paris and then, to please his father, turned to the study of law at Orléans and Bourges (Luther's experience had been the reverse). In about 1533 he experienced a "sudden conversion" and, intent on restoring the church to its original purity, became a Protestant. He escaped imprisonment in Noyon and fled to Basel in 1535. There, at age twenty-six, he wrote the single most influential document of the Protestant Reformation, *Institutes of the Christian Religion,*[13] the textbook of Reformed theology, which he continued to enlarge and revise until 1559, although the doctrinal positions never changed.

In 1536 Calvin moved to Geneva, which became the center of his reforming activity. In a series of "ordinances" issued during the years 1541–1555 he tried to establish there a Christian theocracy, a "holy commonwealth," in which in theory all citizens were members of "the elect" and in which authority was given to "pastors, doctors, elders, and deacons." A "consistory" composed of laymen and clergy functioned as a moral tribunal with power of excommunication and control of the private lives of citizens.

Calvin had no doubt that exile and, in some cases, death were proper penalties for heretics. Between 1542 and 1555, when Calvin was fully in control of Geneva, fifty-eight persons were executed and seventy-six banished. Among the scholars killed after torture the most famous was Michael Servetus (1511–1553), a native of Navarre who became a brilliant physician[14] and theologian whose biblical studies led him to reject the doctrine of the Trinity, holding that the Logos was not fully divine. He had the temerity to return a copy of Calvin's *Institutes* to him with critical comments written in the margins. In a gross miscalculation, Servetus fled from the Inquisition to Geneva, where Calvin promptly had him burned at the stake on October 27, 1555. He died with a prayer to Jesus on his lips.

John Calvin's theology is much more systematic than that of Luther. Reminiscent of the starting point of Islam, the central doctrine for him was the awe-inspiring and fearful majesty of God, who is to be distinguished from all idols. Anything that could divert from the worship of God—stained glass windows, complicated music, statues—was to be eliminated. Absolute obedience to God, bowing before God's inscrutable will, is the duty of all human beings.

According to Calvin, Adam and Eve were created good and capable of obeying God's will. In the fall, however, they lost their goodness, and they and all their descendants fell into a state of ruin that merits nothing but eternal damnation. Some persons are rescued from this hopeless condition through the work of Jesus Christ, who paid the penalty for those who would be saved. Salvation comes only through the work of the Holy Spirit, who creates repentance and faith and effects a union between the believer and Christ. There is therefore no justification by works. But human beings are saved in order to be able to do good works. Therefore justification is not without works, and God's law directs human beings in this regard. Calvinism emphasized the development of good character.

Because all good is from God and humans are unable to initiate or resist conversion, it necessarily follows that the reason not all are saved is God's eternal predestination of some to eternal salvation and the others to eternal damnation (double predestination). We cannot know the mind of God, but we can be sure that this is the case. Calvin's theology fostered absolute certainty of being among the elect and great zeal and energy in implementing what was conceived to be God's will.

The Radical Reformation

A wide variety of groups that pressed for a more radical reform than that of Luther or Calvin emerged at an early period in Reformation history. Because they had in common a rejection of infant baptism, requiring adults to be baptized again, they were widely known as Anabaptists (that is, re-baptizers; the radicals themselves rejected this term and referred to "believers' baptism"). They generally also rejected the slogan "the Bible alone" (*sola scriptura*) and held to continuing revelation through the immediacy of the Holy Spirit. The radicals were the only Reformation groups that held to voluntary membership—the separation of true believers from the non-Christian state. Radicals differed on the proper strategy in the struggle against the evil world. Some, especially in the early period, advocated the use of the sword to establish the kingdom of God on Earth, while most eventually became absolute pacifists.

A notorious example of violent radicalism occurred in the town of Münster, in Germany near the border with the Netherlands. In the early 1530s there were three groups in the city: a small number of Roman Catholics, who supported the bishop; some conservative Lutherans, who were strongly represented in the city council; and—perhaps the majority—followers of Melchior Hofmann, an untutored leather worker and apostate Lutheran who had preached in the area from Strassburg to the Netherlands. The radicals gained control of the city council toward the end of 1533. Then, in February 1534 the prophet John of Leyden appeared in Münster, calling on the common people to rise up in arms, drive out the godless, burn all books except the Bible, and establish the "heavenly Jerusalem." He formed a commune and introduced polygamy. Catholics and Lutherans fled the city, and all who refused adult baptism were banished. Wearing royal robes John began to call himself king of New Zion. He then taught believers that it was their duty to exterminate the ungodly, and his followers slipped out of town, planning uprisings in Dutch towns elsewhere. In May 1535 a few dozen radicals attacked the city hall of Amsterdam during a town banquet, killing the mayor and several leading citizens.

The Lutherans, under Philip of Hesse, and the Catholics now joined military forces. After a long siege, the city of Münster fell on June 25, 1535. The leaders of the commune were tortured to death, and their bodies were placed in iron baskets that hung in the tower of Lambert Church until 1881 (the baskets remained there into the mid-twentieth century). Catholicism was restored in Münster, and for many decades to come the name of the town was enough to destroy all arguments for religious toleration of dissidents.

Apart from the radical fringe, the radicals of the Reformation emphasized pacifism and nonresistance. Among the major groups were the Swiss Brethren, the Hutterite Brethren, the Mennonites, and the anti-Trinitarians.

The Swiss Brethren broke with Zwingli over the doctrine of the church and insisted that a person joins by choice on professing the faith and promising to lead a godly life. The views of this group are summarized in the closest thing to a creed evolved by Anabaptists, the Schleitheim Articles of 1527, the first attempt to unite Anabaptists into one body. From the Swiss came the Amish, who were named after the Mennonite bishop Jakob Ammann (active in the 1690s).

The Hutterite Brethren of Moravia were organized by Jacob Hutter (who was executed in 1536) as thriving spiritual economic communities ("brother houses"). The brethren eschewed individual property but the communities could become prosperous from the manufacture of clocks, tableware, china, and other nonmilitary goods. After the Thirty Years War the Hutterites were expelled from Moravia and moved into Slovakia, Turkey, and the Ukraine. In the 1870s they came to South Dakota and midwestern Canada, where they continue to live.

Menno Simons (1496–1561), a Roman Catholic priest who converted to Protestantism in 1536 after reading Luther's writings, worked fervently to purge Anabaptism of its violent elements after the calamity at Münster. Establishing congregations of "reborn" Christians, he taught that baptism does not confer grace but is a symbol of spiritual rebirth. The Lord's Supper is a memorial of Jesus' death. Only true believers constitute the church, which has the right of excommunication. Service in the state is contrary to the Bible and therefore forbidden. Simons's followers, known as Mennonites, spread through the Low Countries and into northern Germany. The Mennonites flourished in North America, where they are well represented today.

On anti-Trinitarians, like the Socinians, see chapter 10.

The English Break with Rome

Another kind of fissure within Western Christendom occurred in England when King Henry VIII (1491–1547) broke with the Roman church over his desire to have a male heir. The least theological of the Reformations, it essentially involved the establishing of a national church in the 1530s without significant doctrinal changes.

Henry's actions followed previous moves toward a national church. In the 1350s, Parliament had limited taxes that could be paid to the pope, then residing in France. In addition, both Wycliffe and Occam had developed theological critiques of the papacy. But without Henry's marital problems, the Church of England might not have been born.

Henry's marriages and the complicated relationships of the monarchs of England, Spain, and the Holy Roman Empire are best diagramed:

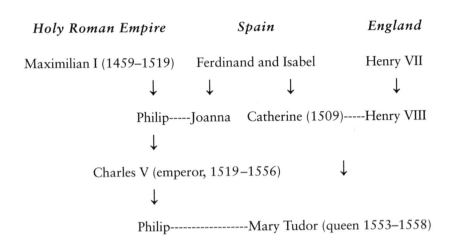

Holy Roman Empire   *Spain*   *England*

Maximilian I (1459–1519)   Ferdinand and Isabel   Henry VII
         ↓   ↓   ↓   ↓

              Philip-----Joanna   Catherine (1509)-----Henry VIII
                   ↓

Charles V (emperor, 1519–1556)   ↓

              Philip------------------Mary Tudor (queen 1553–1558)

Other wives of Henry VIII:
Anne Boleyn, mother of Elizabeth (queen 1558–1603)
Jane Seymour, mother of Edward (king 1547–1553)
Anne of Cleves
Catherine Howard
Catherine Parr, the only wife to survive Henry

When Catherine of Aragon, daughter of Ferdinand and Isabel, bore Henry only one daughter, Henry appealed to the pope for an annullment based on the "impediment" that Catherine had earlier been married to Henry's brother Arthur, who had died shortly after the marriage. The pope, however, feared antagonizing Catherine's nephew, Charles V, who in 1527 had attacked Rome. Henry then turned to the anti-papal party in England, especially Thomas Cromwell and Thomas Cranmer. Working with "the reforming Parliament" of 1529 to 1536, these men accomplished the break with Rome.

In 1533 Parliament abolished papal authority in England, and Cranmer, after being appointed archbishop of Canterbury, the highest office in the Church of England, declared Henry's marriage to Catherine invalid. In 1534 Parliament passed the Supremacy Act, in which the monarch was declared "the only supreme head [this term was later change to 'governor'] in earth of the church of England." (The doctrine that the civil ruler is also the head of the church in the nation is known as Erastianism.) Rome excommunicated Henry in 1535. In the following year Henry made his most radical move—confiscating the property of 376 monasteries, which he gave to the nobles in an attempt to strengthen the throne.

When Henry died in 1547 there were three religious parties in England. The largest group stood with Henry, wanting little change and no foreign control. A small group remained faithfully Roman Catholic. Small Protestant groups, in contrast, pressed for reforms like those on the continent.

Henry VIII's only surviving son, ten-year-old Edward, became king at Henry's death, with the government run by a council. During this time Thomas Cranmer published the first edition of the *Book of Common Prayer,* which remains to this day the strongest bond between groups within the Anglican Communion. Cranmer also composed a doctrinal statement for the church, the Forty-two Articles.

Upon Edward's death in 1553, Mary Tudor took the throne (1553–1558) and brought the country back to Roman Catholicism, beginning a period of persecution of Protestants. Her chief enemy was Thomas Cranmer, architect of the Church of England and the man who had declared her mother's marriage invalid. Cranmer was burned at the stake on March 21, 1556.

Henry's only other surviving child, Elizabeth, reigned from 1558 to 1603, a golden age in English history. The Roman position that her birth was illegitimate made it a foregone conclusion that she would support the Protestants. During her reign the Church of England took permanent shape—the "Elizabethan settlement"—with another Supremacy Act in which the monarch was declared "the supreme governor" of the church, a revision of the *Book of Common Prayer,* and the revision of the Forty-two Articles into the Thirty-nine Articles.

England remained aloof from the Thirty Years War (1618–1648) and witnessed during this time a proliferation of sects. The Church of England was established, but there were also Presbyterians (Calvinists), Independents (Congregationalists), Baptists, Quakers, Unitarians, and Roman Catholics. How could these groups coexist? Or could they? How much tolerance could there be in a church-state system? Parliament in 1689 answered the question in the Act of Toleration: The Church of England is established, and the Thirty-nine Articles would be required of all groups, except those which would not permit their existence. (Presbyterians, for example, were exempt from the article on polity and Baptists from the article on infant baptism.) But there was not yet toleration for Roman Catholics and Unitarians. A milestone in church development had nonetheless been passed.

The Roman Reformation (Counter-Reformation)

Occupying the papacy when the Reformation broke out were Italian princes who patronized renaissance art but did not understand the implications of the Reformation. Within fifty years of the time of Luther, however, the Roman church had corrected many of the abuses that prompted the Reformation. In addition, new religious orders had arisen to combat Protestantism. The Calvinist areas bore the brunt of the Roman attack, which was most effective in Spain and Italy. The Roman Reformation had three prongs: new orders such as the Jesuits, the renewed Inquisiton, and the Council of Trent.

The Jesuits

Among the new orders that arose in opposition to Protestantism—the Theatines, Sommaschi, Barnabites, Capuchins, and others—the chief instrument of the Counter-Reformation was the Jesuits. Their founder, Ignatius Loyola (1491–1556), was wounded and crippled for life in 1521 as an officer in the Spanish army. He turned to reading the lives of the saints and determined to devote his life as a soldier to the Virgin Mary. During a time of spiritual struggle he formulated his famous *Spiritual Exercises,* a month-long discipline designed to make one aware of the damnable nature of sin and to incorporate into oneself the life, sufferings, death, resurrection, and ascension of Jesus—a dramatizing of the Gospels patterned after military training. The *Exercises* led to a high degree of self-discipline and religious idealism.

Ignatius went to Jerusalem in 1523 hoping to convert Muslims. He decided, however, that he could do nothing without a good theological education. After studying in Barcelona and Salamanca, he went to Paris in 1528, where he gathered a group of friends who took vows of poverty and chastity and bound themselves to go to the Holy Land. The group took the name Society of Jesus (Jesuits) in 1537 and was approved by a papal bull of September 1540.

The Jesuits set for themselves ambitious goals. They founded schools to educate the young. To gain the masses back to Rome, they emphasized preaching on the essentials of faith, catechetical instructution, and secured access to the important courts of Europe. They were highly active in world missions. Francis Xavier (1506–1552) traveled to Goa in India, where a Portuguese colony existed until the mid-twentieth century. He traveled through East Asia and died in China. Other Jesuits worked in South America, Central America, and parts of North America.

The Renewed Inquisition

Gradually realizing that Western Christendom was being split, the papal court was divided on how to deal with the situation. Some members—usually supporting them were the French and the emperor Charles V—thought that reform of both doctrine and discipline would allow Protestants to return to the Roman church. In contrast, the closest advisors of the popes, supported by the Spanish, favored strong measures against heresy. The latter group won the day, having been especially prompted by Cardinal Caraffa (1476–1559), who became Pope Paul IV (1555–1559). A papal bull of July 21, 1542 reorganized the Inquisition largely on the Spanish model that had worked so effectively in the previous century. The Inquisition now was limited in practice to areas where political leaders allowed it to function. Protestantism thus was practically wiped out of Spain and Italy; thousands were put to death.

In 1908 the Inquisition's name was changed to the Congregation of the Holy Office and, in 1917, it was given charge of the Index of Prohibited Books. Its functions were abolished by Vatican II in the 1960s.

The Council of Trent

Already in 1519 Luther had demanded that a general church council hear his case. Tensions between the emperor and the papacy as well as uncertainty about the gravity of the situation prevented a council from being held until 1545, when the bishops gathered at Trent, in the southern tip of Austria (at that time a part of the empire, although on the southern side of the Alps). By this time there was little chance of undoing the Reformation; Lutherans refused to attend, and Luther—a year before his death—wrote his most violent tract on the papacy, *Against Roman Popery Founded by the Devil*.

Trent met in three assemblies. In the first assembly, 1545–1547, the first issue was the question of which would be discussed first— matters of doctrine or reform? Charles V pressed for reform matters in the hope that Protestants might be brought in, but the papacy wanted doctrine to be defined first. A compromise that both would be discussed simultaneously meant that Protestants were alienated. Most of the important anti-Protestant doctrinal decisions of Trent were made during the first assembly:

- Scripture and tradition are equally authoritative standards of divine revelation. Jerome's Vulgate (Latin Bible) is the authoritative text (contra Protestant translations into the vernaculars), and the church (with the pope as head) has the sole right to interpret it. *Sola scriptura* is excluded.
- Original sin as inherited from Adam is affirmed, although human beings are not "wholly depraved." Not sin itself but the consequence of sin is retained by all human beings.
- On justification—the central doctrine for most Protestants— Trent issued thirty-seven canons that condemned Protestant views. God calls the adult through prevenient grace, without human merit, but grace is possible by the merits and sufferings of

Christ. In addition, justification involves not only forgiveness but also sanctification—a process of renewal in life.

- Seven sacraments (the ones identified by Thomas) are necessary for human salvation (although not everyone needs all seven). All except baptism can be performed only by clergy (contra the Protestant emphasis on the priesthood of all believers).

Although some Lutherans attended the second assembly, 1551–1552, the effect was to demonstrate how wide was the chasm between them and the Roman church. This assembly formulated the dogma on several sacraments, including the Eucharist (understood as a sacrifice), penance, and extreme unction (last rites).

The third assembly took place in 1562–1563. Recognizing the permanence of the break with the Protestants, the pope prepared to counteract the Protestants and to regain what had been lost. This assembly defined the sacraments of ordination and marriage, the doctrine of indulgences, and the Index of Prohibited Books. Finally, the council declared that all prior decrees of the council were binding on the faithful.

In 1564 Pope Pius IV issued a bull, *Injunctum nobis,* that summarized the decrees of the Council of Trent: Scripture plus traditon; seven sacraments; Eucharist as sacrifice; the existence of purgatory; veneration of saints; the power of indulgences; obedience to the pope. This summary of faith is required of all converts to Roman Catholicism.

The Council of Trent signified Roman Catholic acceptance of the *fact* of Protestantism and left the Roman church much more unified in doctrine than it had been at the start of the century.

The English Bible

One of the lasting results of the Protestant Reformation was the translation of the Bible into the language of the common people (the vernacular). The language of the European churches prior to the sixteenth century was Latin, and many prominent leaders in church and state feared that making the Bible available to the masses would lead to insubordination and heresy. So strongly and widely held was this fear that the act of translating often brought with it the real possibility of torture and execution.

The first complete translation of the Bible into English—from the Latin text (the "Vulgate") instead of the original Hebrew and Greek—was done by the proto-reformer John Wycliffe and his followers in the 1380s. Church authorities condemned this work as "the crown of wickedness" and threatened excommunication for anyone who read it or produced another such work. Despite being a translation of a translation, Wycliffe's work influenced subsequent English translations of the Bible.

Two events of the fifteenth century greatly facilitated translators of the Bible. When Constantinople, the capital of the Eastern (Greek) empire, fell to the Turkish Muslims in 1453, many of its scholars fled to the West, bringing with them their knowledge of the Greek language and the Greek classical tradition. Thus Erasmus in 1516 published one of the first critical editions of the Greek text of the New Testament, which was used both by Martin Luther and by William Tyndale. The other event was the development of the movable-type printing press by Johann Gutenberg in the middle of the fifteenth century, without which the Reformation and the dissemination of Bible translations would have been much more difficult.

Few lives in church history are more dramatic than that of William Tyndale (ca. 1494–1536).[15] A gifted linguist, Tyndale for his work of translation had at his disposal the complete Old Testament in Hebrew and Erasmus's edition of the Greek New Testament. Facing life-threatening opposition in England, especially from Thomas More, Tyndale published the first edition of his translation of the New Testament in 1525 at Cologne. He worked also at Worms and spent the last years of his life at Antwerp, translating large parts of the Old Testament there. His was the first English translation of the Bible to be made from the original Hebrew and Greek and also the first (with the Old Testament incomplete) to be printed. For his efforts, however, he was betrayed by acquaintances, condemned as a heretic, and burned at the stake on October 6, 1536, at the castle of Vilvorde, near Brussels. But his work was largely incorporated in all subsequent English translations of the Bible. It is striking that in the King James Version 84 percent of the words of the New Testament and nearly 76 percent of those in the Old Testament are from Tyndale's work.[16]

Between Tyndale and the King James Version of 1611 several new versions of the English Bible were published. Miles Coverdale's work appeared in 1535 and that of Thomas Matthew (pseudonym for John Rogers) in 1537. In 1539 the "Great Bible," a revision of Coverdale's, was published in England (the religious currents in London were changing, owing to the machinations of Henry VIII). When Henry's daughter Mary became queen of England in 1553, many Protestants fled to Geneva where, in 1560, they published the Geneva Bible, based largely on Tyndale's work; this was the Bible of Shakespeare, John Bunyan, and the Puritans. A replacement of the Great Bible, the so-called Bishops' Bible, was published in 1568. Then, in 1582 and 1609, Roman Catholic refugees in France and Flanders published an English translation of the Latin Bible, a work known as the Douay or Rheims-Douay version.

In February 1604 King James I of England ordered "that a translation be made of the whole Bible, as consonant as can be to the original Hebrew and Greek; and this to be set out and printed without any marginal notes, and only to be used in all churches of England in time of divine service."[17] The labor of fifty-four translators resulted in the publication in 1611 of what came to be known as the King James Version or the "Authorized Version" (but there is no evidence that it was authorized by the church or by the British Parliament). After gaining widespread use by the middle of the seventeenth century, this magnificent translation maintained a place of honor among English-speaking peoples, with no serious proposal for revisions, for two and a half centuries. It not only improved the work of Tyndale but, in its classic cadences, some have thought that it improved the style of the original Greek of the New Testament itself.[18]

Conclusion

During the sixteenth century the unity of Western Christendom was permanently shattered and the precedent for religious pluralism securely established. Although the Reformers were dominated by religious and theological matters, the upheaval they set in motion opened the door to new ideas. The subsequent centuries would see the increase of nationalism, rationalism, the beginnings of classical music, geographical exploration, scientific discovery, and much else. They also would be a time of competing approaches to truth.

10

ORTHODOXISM, PIETISM, AND RATIONALISM

The Crisis of Competing Truth-Claims

Let us remember that in the last judgment we shall not be asked how learned we were and whether we displayed our learning before the world; to what extent we enjoyed the favor of men and knew how to keep it; with what honors we were exalted and how great a reputation in the world we left behind us or how many treasure of earthly goods we amassed for our children and thereby drew a curse upon ourselves. Instead, we shall be asked how faithfully and with how childlike a heart we sought to further the kingdom of God; with how pure and godly a teaching and how worthy an example we tried to edify our hearers amid the scorn of the world, denial of self, taking up of the cross, and imitation of our Savior; with what zeal we opposed not only error but also wickedness of life; or with what constancy and cheerfulness we endured the persecution or adversity thrust upon us by the manifestly godless world or by false brethren, and amid such suffering praised our God.

—Philip Jacob Spener, *Pia Desideria*, 1675[1]

The issue: Which of three competing varieties of Christian thought and piety would prevail?

Modernism refers to the attitudes and ideas associated with the kind of optimistic rationality that seeks to discover the laws of nature, abolish outmoded ways of thought, and lead to a better life for humanity on Earth. With respect to the history of Christianity, modernity in the West emerged in the post-Reformation period out of the ascendancy, although not the absolute hegemony, of rationalism over the other two main approaches to religious life and belief, orthodoxism and pietism. Although modernity and the certainties that accompanied it have come into disrepute in our postmodern intellectual climate, the heirs of these three kinds of piety are still much in evidence today.

Orthodoxism

In the generations following the work of the great reformers, theologians worked at systematizing their doctrines. In the clash with the Roman church, Protestants had emphasized the supreme authority of the Bible. Orthodoxist theologians now often claimed to derive "pure doctrine" from an inerrant Bible directly inspired word-for-word by the Holy Spirit. The results were predictable: each Protestant tradition or "confession" published theological systems that were at odds with those of other groups. The orthodoxist approach is therefore anti-ecumenical by nature.

The orthodoxist period is one of partisanship, religious war, and economic stagnation. During the years 1580 to 1700 the population of Germany was reduced from eighteen million to ten million. James H. Nichols describes the situation thus:

> The fields were barren, cattle stolen or killed, homes destroyed, and commerce paralyzed. The cultural and moral degradation was comparable. A whole generation grew up in the lawlessness of warfare. Wild children roamed in packs; thousands of women were debauched; education virtually disappeared.[2]

In the midst of calamitous suffering, great theological systems and, perhaps more surprising, classic hymns and devotional literature were produced.

Philip Melanchthon

Martin Luther was more a creative spiritual genius than a systematic theologian. His right-hand man, Philipp Melanchthon (1497–1560) was in some respects a precursor of Lutheran orthodoxism. Educated at Heidelberg and Tübingen, he came to Wittenberg 1518 at the age of twenty-one as a professor of Greek. There he came under Luther's influence and took part in the Leipzig debates, the 1529 Diet of Speyer, and the 1529 Marburg Colloquy. In 1521 he wrote the first edition of his summary of faith, the *Loci Communes,* and for the 1530 Diet of Augsburg he wrote the *Augsburg Confession,* which remains to this day the most universal doctrinal confession of Lutherans around the world.

Melanchthon was a peace-loving, quiet person who worked to heal the breach with the Roman church as well as with the Greek church. It is therefore ironic that after Luther's death (at which he preached the funeral sermon) he was embroiled in a series of doctrinal controversies between Philippists (who claimed to follow him) and Gnesio-Lutherans (genuine Lutherans, a minority group). In this situation some differences of approach between Luther and Melanchthon emerged.

- Melanchthon had less interest than Luther in Christian freedom and more on Christian holiness.
- Melanchthon made less of a distinction than did Luther between the word of God and the Bible. For Luther the word of God is seen especially in the person and work of Jesus.
- If Luther called human reason a "great whore" as a source of truth, Melanchthon had respect for Aristotle and could speak of reason and revelation as twin sources of truth.
- Melanchthon emphasized sound doctrine; for Luther the center of Christianity was the experience of God's grace.
- Melanchthon, much more than Luther, taught that justification by faith leads to regeneration—transformation of character, the ability to keep God's law.
- Melanchthon valued Christian tradition more highly than did Luther. He believed that the consensus of the first four or five

centuries of Christian theology could be considered determinative for Christian unity at any period.

Many of these and other differences were settled for Lutherans by
the Formula of Concord of 1577, which was included in the *Book of
Concord* (1580), the complete collection of Lutheran confessions.[3]

Johann Gerhard (1583–1637)

Johann Gerhard is the most important theologian of Lutheran
orthodoxy. His *Loci* of 1622 covers four thousand pages of
small type. Between the consideration of sacred Scripture and a
final chapter on eternal life, Gerhard examines every aspect of
Christian thought and speculation—a complete statement of Lutheran doctrine against Roman Catholics, other Protestants, and secular thinkers.

Gerhard's attitude toward the Bible is typical of his approach.
According to Gerhard, God determined that revelation should be
committed to writing in order to preserve it in a pure state through
all future time, establish concord in the church, provide a summary
of the faith for secular authorities, and distinguish heretics from true
believers. The terms "Bible" and "word of God" are completely syn-
onymous; there is no word of God to be found anywhere else. Moreover, the Bible contains the word of God entirely and completely.
There has been no unwritten word of God since the publication of
the canon. The Bible therefore is unlike any other book: God is the
principal cause of it while the human authors are only the instru-
mental cause. God communicated both the form and the content, so
that every detail in the Bible is completely free from error on every
subject it touches.[4] The Bible has four attributes:

- *Authority.* The Bible has causative authority in creating and
  confirming in the human mind assent to the truths it teaches,
  and it has normative authority as the sole norm to settle all theological disputes.
- *Perfection or sufficiency.* All the contents of the Bible are true,
  and they are all that we need to know and believe for salvation.

- *Perspicuity (clarity)*. The contents of the Bible are accessible to human understanding—at least the parts that are necessary for salvation. Mature judgment, philological training, and an unprejudiced mind are required.
- *Efficacy.* The Bible is the means for the communication of divine power to illumine, convert, and justify.

In short, the authority of the Bible as the source of doctrine is rational and logical, and the theory of its inspiration was treated mechanistically. Some thought it blasphemous to suggest that the Greek of the New Testament was less than perfect; that would be to accuse the Holy Spirit of being unable to write properly.

Because orthodoxist theologians generally had a higher regard for philosophy (such as that of Aristotle and the scholastics) and church tradition than did the reformers, they tended to consider the whole content of revelation as a conglomeration of propositions, sometimes called articles of faith. These propositions or articles can be collected in a book, such as, for Lutherans, the *Book of Concord*. Such "confessions" might be considered mediately revealed, while the Bible comes through immediate revelation.

Pietism

Both pietism and rationalism can be seen as reactions to orthodoxism. Tending toward individual autonomy in matters of faith, they both objected to orthodoxist dalliance with clericalism (sacerdotalism, or a separate class of priests), scholasticism, denominationalism, traditionalism, and creedalism. Beyond these commonalities, however, they differed greatly on what constitutes true religion.

Pietism was a reaction against orthodoxism that emphasized the personal experience of religious truth (adult conversion), devotional life, moral discipline, an ascetic attitude toward the world, and the active role of laypersons (the "priesthood of all believers") in the upbuilding of Christian life. The movement crossed confessional lines, reaching also into Roman Catholic areas.

Antecedents of pietism can be found in the works of some medieval mystics, including the Dominican Johann Tauler (ca. 1300–1361) and the anonymous late fourteenth-century mystical treatise *Theologia Germanica,* the first printing of which was instigated by Martin Luther in 1518.[5] Also, during the orthodoxist period appeared *True Christianity* (1606) by Johann Arndt (1555–1621), which emphasized the atonement as the work of Christ in the human heart, and the abstruse devotional and mystical writings of Jakob Boehme (1575–1624), who influenced German and English philosophers as well as the Quakers.

Philip Jacob Spener (1635–1705)

The beginnings of pietism proper, however, are found in the work of Philip Jacob Spener, who became a pastor in Frankfurt-am-Main in 1666. Concerned to renew the spiritual life of his people, he began a practice that was to be widespread in pietism—the *collegia pietatis* (from which comes the term "pietist") or conventicles, small groups that gathered in homes for Bible study, prayer, spiritual discipline, and discussion of the Sunday sermon. In 1675 Spener published what came to be the guidebook for pietism, *Pia desideria* (Pious longings), a plea for the renewal of personal religion on the basis of Luther's principles.[6] In this little book Spener emphasized the need for conversion as a conscious experience, called for the study of the Bible by all classes of Christians, encouraged all believers to act as priests to others, exercising mutual love and service, and to reject all religious controversy, dealing with heretics in a spirit of love. Theological professors should be examples of piety, and seminarians trained in piety as well as in doctrine. Preaching should be simple and aimed at changing the heart as well as the mind.

At least as he saw it, Spener's theology was orthodox Lutheran, and he made no attack on the theology of his time. But his theological attitude was enormously different from that of most of his contemporaries. According to Spener, only when the conduct of one's life is actually changed can one claim to be born again. Activities the orthodoxists considered *adiaphora* (indifferent matters), such as theater, dance, card playing, and alcohol, were to be avoided. For Spener, the Reformation had not completed its work. Purification of doctrine had to be followed by purification of life. He effected a shift from creeds to Scripture, from head to heart, and from intellect to emotion and experience. The University of Wittenberg accused him of two hundred errors and heresies, but his influence lived on.

August Hermann Francke (1663–1727)

In 1687, while preparing a sermon on John 20:31 ("These are written so that you may come to believe that Jesus is the Messiah, the Son of God, and that through believing you may have life in his name"), August Hermann Francke suddenly saw his entire past life rise before him in a void of inner darkness. He prayed in anguish until peace finally came. From that time on he was zealous for God and willing to suffer anything for God's cause. He organzied Bible study groups at Leipzig but was driven out of town by the authorities. He attracted large crowds in Erfurt but in 1691 was forced to leave there also.

Francke moved to the University of Halle, where he preached and lectured from 1694 to 1727. Each year eight to twelve hundred theology students attended his classes. His Canstein Institute distributed three million Bibles by the end of the eighteenth century. He founded schools for all classes of children—an innovation. The orphanage he started in Halle with meager funds grew into a chain of charitable institutions throughout Germany—hospitals, dispensaries, almshouses, and much else, many of which exist to this day.

Francke's other passionate interest was world missions. If the orthodoxists had a distaste for such,[7] Francke looked to the ends of the earth and began the tradition of Protestant missionizing. Securing funds from the king of Denmark, he began mission work in South India. Later, hearing reports of German colonists in Pennsylvania without spiritual direction, he sent Henry Melchior Muhlenberg to organize the Lutheran church in North America. Francke's lasting contribution to pietism was his emphasis on social work and world missions.

Nicholas Ludwig von Zinzendorf (1700–1760) and the Moravians

Pietism at times led to new church structures. In the early 1700s Hussites from Moravia—an illegal, persecuted group—began to seek refuge in Saxony. In 1722 Count Nicholas Ludwig von Zinzendorf, a pietist influenced by Francke, allowed them to form a village, which they called Herrnhut, on his estate. This community attracted large numbers of pietists and soon adopted a system of elders and bishops—the beginning of the Moravian church. The first bishop was ordained in 1735. Although Zinzendorf had advised them to remain a force within the state Lutheran church, the Moravians wanted to create a purified and separate church body. Herrnhut was to be a commune apart from the world (children, for example, were separated from their parents and raised jointly), but ready to work in the world as soldiers for Christ. The Moravians soon displayed a passion for world missions, the work of which was largely supported by the king of Denmark. Moravians did mission work in difficult places such Guiana, Egypt, south and central Africa, Labrador, and among Native Americans.

Charged by orthodoxists and other pietists with separatism and proselytizing, Zinzendorf was banished from Saxony in 1736. After being ordained a Moravian bishop in 1737, he went to London and the West Indies and then, in 1747, to the American colonies, where he founded the American headquarters for the Moravian church in the town he named Bethlehem, in Pennsylvania. Although Zinzendorf never abandoned the idea of working within the larger church, his efforts to unite all German Protestants in America into one church body failed.

Nearly bankrupt, Zinzendorf spent his last years doing pastoral work at Herrnhut; he died there May 1760. He retained to the end a peculiar intense emotional piety that centered on the blood and wounds of Christ and sometimes used erotic imagery.[8] But at the time of his death the Moravian Church was firmly established.

John Wesley (1703–1791) and the Methodists

The Methodist Church, which grew out of the work of John Wesley, is the single largest institutional result of pietism. Unlike other pietistic movements, it began as a reaction against rationalism, not orthodoxism. In England in 1700 it was fashionable to present Christianity as a moral system with divine sanctions. Social conditions were at a low ebb, vulgarity was common, and justice severe. The Industrial Revolution was beginning—during Wesley's lifetime were invented the spinning machine, the power loom, and the steam engine—and life was harsh for the lower classes, who were all but excluded from the church. In this situation religious societies for the promotion of piety and aid to the poor, soldiers, and prisoners sprang up. In 1700 there were one hundred such societies in London alone, one of them founded by Sam Wesley, John's father. The great hymnwriter and theologian Isaac Watts (1674–1748) shared many of Sam Wesley's concerns.

John Wesley, born in 1703, was the fifteenth of eighteen children; his brother Charles, a great hymnwriter, was born in 1707. They both escaped death in a fire in 1709, and John would later refer to himself as a "brand snatched from the burning." Raised in a strict and pious home, the brothers studied at Oxford. John was graduated with honors and, in 1725, ordained a deacon in the Church of England and a chosen a fellow of Lincoln College at Oxford. He was ordained a priest in 1728. In 1729 John, Charles, and some friends formed at Oxford a religious society to foster piety, fasting, and the reading of the mystics. Oxford students mocked them as "the Holy Club" and, because of their steady habits, as "methodists"—an epithet that stuck.

Both Wesleys went to America in 1735 to a new colony founded by James Edward Oglethorpe—Georgia. During the sea passage and again in Georgia, John Wesley came into contact with Moravians who pressed him about his personal assurance of salvation. In Georgia the Wesleys worked hard, preaching and opposing the slave trade, but with little success. In 1736 Charles returned to England in ill health and disappointment. John stayed on and began a relationship with a woman, but was not able to decide between clerical celibacy and marriage. Altercations between the woman's family and Wesley were part of the reason he returned to England, depressed, fearing death, and unsure of his faith.

In London he again came into contact with Moravians, who taught instantaneous conversion and joy in believing. Finally, on May 24, 1738, at Aldersgate Street in London, while listening to a reading of Luther's "Preface to Romans," he experienced a kind of conversion.

> About a quarter before nine, while [Luther] was describing the change that God works in the heart through faith in Christ, I felt my heart strangely warmed. I felt I did trust in Christ, Christ alone, for my salvation, and an assurance was given me that he had taken away my sins, even mine, and saved me from the law of sin and death.[9]

From that time until his death, John Wesley worked with tremendous energy, especially among the working classes of England. He averaged eight thousand miles on horseback each year, wrote thousands of letters, and preached countless sermons. Because the church doors were often closed to him and although he considered it a vile innovation, he preached outdoors to large crowds of people—to coal miners, prisoners, and the poor in the fields. In addition, like all other pietists, he established small groups, "classes," of twelve people each to meet each week to inquire into the spiritual and moral welfare of the members.

The Methodist movement began to grow also in America. Although Wesley himself wanted the movement to remain within the Anglican Church, he ordained the Welshman Thomas Coke as superintendent or bishop for work in the colonies and instructed him to ordain Francis Asbury in America as his colleague. By Wesley's death in 1791 the movement was established.

John Wesley was gifted in courage, leadership, preaching, piety, and charity. Although Methodism was not primarily a theological movement, it proved to be a spawner of splinter groups. For example, Wesley's emphasis on "another birth" influenced the development in the United States in the 1800s of the Holiness Churches with their "baptism in the Spirit," which in turn influenced the Pentecostal churches of the early 1900s and the charismatic movements of the late 1900s.

American Revivalism

The typical form of American pietism was—and is—revivalism. In the early years there were two outbreaks of revivalism: the Great Awakening of 1740–1743 associated with Jonathan Edwards (1703–1758) and the Second Awakening of 1795–1830 associated in the east with Timothy Dwight (1752–1817) of Yale College and in the west with "camp meetings."

As the Great Awakening began, only 10 percent of Americans were church members. The movement began after Edwards's conversion in 1727 and his work as a Congregational minister in Northampton, Massachusetts. Central to Edwards's work was a passionate Calvinism, which he articulated in several books and in sermons such as "Sinners in the Hands of an Angry God." Repulsed by the "licentious" behavior of the young people in the town, including the mirth and jollity of "the frolics" in which both sexes partied into the night, he began to meet with them in their homes. His church sermons emphasized justification by faith alone and attacked religious indifference. Conversions began. Owing to the efforts of Edwards and his associate George Whitefield (1714–1770), the Great Awakening spread from New England through every colony from Nova Scotia to Georgia, reaching all classes, rich and poor. Besides the renewal of religious life and the weakening of denominational hostilities, the movement initiated many charitable projects, such as schools for Native Americans, aid to slaves, and the founding of colleges and universities.

The Second Awakening began at Yale in 1795 when Timothy Dwight, grandson of Jonathan Edwards, became president there. Dwight preached against materialism and "infidelity" (by which he usually meant deism, a generic belief in God without a specific Christology). The eastern revival was dignified and quiet and in 1802 one-third of the students at Yale professed conversion.

The western phase of the Second Awakening was far different from the eastern. Revivals there spread like wildfire—camp meetings marked by "spectacular manifestations" befitting the wild frontier, including jerkings, trances, rolling on the ground, the "holy laugh," and such. One of the largest of the camp meetings was held in

August 1801 at Cane Ridge near Lexington, Kentucky; it drew some twenty thousand persons.

American revivals proved to be an effective recruiting technique for the churches involved. At the time of the Revolutionary War, the Congregationalists were the largest and most influential religious body in the country, established by law in Massachusetts, Connecticut, and New Hampshire. Next in size were the Presbyterians, followed by Baptists, Episcopalians (out of favor because of the war), Quakers, Reformed, Lutherans, and small numbers of Roman Catholics and Methodists. By 1850 the Methodists were the largest, with 1,324,000 members, followed by Baptists, Presbyterians, Congregationalists, Lutherans, Disciples of Christ, and Episcopalians. Participation in revivals on the part of Methodists and Baptists goes far to explain these amazing statistics.

Pietism in its various forms had salutary effects, especially in the area of social welfare. The movement generally improved the moral conditions of society and fostered ecumenical cooperation. It greatly increased the involvement of laypersons in the work of the church. At the same time, however, its distinction between the once-born and the twice-born carried with it the potential for fanaticism and legalism. Some pietists withdrew from political and other "worldly" pursuits.

Rationalism

Rationalism as a post-Reformation movement can be defined as a reaction against orthodoxism that emphasized doctrines that were considered accessible to universal human reason. A theological aspect of the Enlightenment, the movement espoused toleration, the goodness of human nature, the value of scientific inquiry, human happiness in this world, inevitable progress, and human freedom.

One of the roots of rationalism was the anti-Trinitarian movement of the Reformation period, led by people such as Michael Servetus. The most significant of these was Socinianism, founded by Italians from Siena—Lelio Francesco Maria Sozini (Socinius) (1525–1562) and his nephew Fausto Paolo Sozzini (he added a second z to his name; 1539–1604). By the late sixteenth century the movement was centered in Poland, where the group published its *Racovian Catechism* in 1605. This catechism teaches that the Bible contains revelation and that the purpose of religion is to lead to eternal life. Jesus was a man rewarded for his perfect life by being raised from the dead. Baptism and the Eucharist have symbolic value, but original sin and predestination must be rejected. Jesus' death is neither the satisfaction of an angry God nor vicarious suffering for the sins of others, which would be gross injustice, but a great example of obedience. Human beings have free will, even in matters of church and religion. Socinianism influenced the Unitarian movement in America, as can been seen from the great sermons of William Ellery Channing (1780–1842) in Boston.

Another antecedent or early form of rationalism was the religious orientation of Lord Herbert of Cherbury (Edward Herbert; 1583–1648), a politician, traveler, musician, philosopher, and theologian. Denying that there is divine revelation in a book, he argued that five ideas are innate to all religions and constitute the essence of all true religion: (1) there is a God; (2) God deserves our worship; (3) worship centers on moral virtue; (4) repentance for sin is a duty; (5) there is a future life of rewards and punishments. This approach characterizes all later Deists.

It is helpful to distinguish three kinds of rationalists—rational supernaturalists, Christian Deists, and anti-Christian Deists—by their attitudes toward revealed religion and traditional Christianity.

Rational supernaturalists allowed room for scriptural revelation. In addition to the Socinians, included here is John Tillotson (1630–1694), the archbishop of Canterbury, who viewed religion as a system of rational propositions to be tested by human reason. The function of such propositions is to inculcate morality, to teach us about the existence of God, and to advise us of future rewards and punishments. Revelation is attested by agreement with rational religion, fulfilled prophecies, and the miracles of Jesus.[10]

The English philosopher John Locke (1632–1704) is famous in the history of philosophy for his *Essay Concerning Human Understanding* (1690), in which he treats the human mind as a *tabula rasa*, a blank sheet on which sense impressions are combined into ideas, which are therefore natural and reasonable. In the treatise *Reason-ableness of Christianity as Delivered in the Scriptures* (1695), he suggests that there are three kinds of religious ideas: (1) those according to reason, such as the existence of one God; (2) those above reason but not contradictory to it, which are dependent on revelation, such as the resurrection; and (3) those contrary to reason, such as polytheism, which must be rejected. That the Bible contains revelation, he thought, was proved by the miracles it attests.

Christian Deists rejected the idea or at least the importance of biblical revelation and held essentially the same perspective as that of Herbert of Cherbury, except that they considered themselves followers of Jesus uncontaminated by later accretions and had no specific anti-Christian agenda. Included here are Gottfried Wilhelm Leibniz (1646–1715), a nominal Lutheran who rejected the idea of divine intervention in the world ("All is for the best in this best of all possible worlds") and his popularizer, Christian Wolff (1679–1754). Wolff influenced the early biblical critic J. S. Semler (1725–1791), who relativized biblical authority by treating the New Testament canon as a purely historical question and by insisting that the pure word of God consists of those parts of the Bible that lead to moral improvement. In England, the great Isaac Newton (1642–1727), in *Principia Mathematica* (1687), conceived of the universe as a perpetual motion machine; like the Deists he affirmed belief in God but not in the Trinity. And Matthew Tindal (1655–1733), in *Christianity as Old as the Creation* (1730), specifically called himself a "Christian Deist."

Such views were passionately expounded in Prussia by the great philosopher of Scottish descent, Immanuel Kant (1724–1804), in *Religion within the Limits of Reason Alone* (1793).[11] Kant uses the term religion to denote the one, true, universal system of belief, and the term faith to denote a particular church or denomination. The true religion is an ideal community comprised of all who live according to moral reason—the moral ideas innate to all human beings. This is what Jesus meant by saying, "the kingdom of God is among you" (Luke 17:21–22). This kingdom is ideal, because it is not yet fully implemented.

According to Kant, Christianity began with Jesus teaching a moral religion in accord with reason. But its first founders made historical elements into essential articles of faith, thus corrupting and relativizing the movement.

"Ecclesiastical faith," Kant asserts, is the vehicle for pure religion, which must have a means to preserve its identity everywhere in the same form. Tradition, which changes, cannot do this, but the Bible can. The Bible provides training for the masses, even though it contains much that is superfluous to religion (miracles, eschatology, historical reports). The sole function of biblical interpretation is to foster moral improvement: "I raise the question as to whether morality should be expounded according to the Bible or whether the Bible should not rather be expounded according to morality."[12] Scripture can never be the prerogative of offical scholars of the church, nor can it ever be used against reason. Common people, Kant opines, tend to sink into passive belief and need Scripture as a kind of crutch. Learned persons, however, have less need for revelation.

One attempt to institutionalize Kant's religious ideas is the Society for Ethical Culture, founded in the United States by Felix Adler in 1876. Today, centered in New York City, it continues to support civil liberties, civil rights, and social justice.

Less widely known are the religious views of Thomas Jefferson (1743–1826), who was careful to express them only to trusted friends in private correspondence. These letters, however, leave no doubt that, for Jefferson, Deism was the only true form of Chrsitianity. It is therefore difficult to decide whether Jefferson should be classified as a Chirstian Deist or a non-Christian Deist. Consider his letter of June 26, 1822 to Dr. Benjamin Waterhouse:

> I have received and read with thankfulness and pleasure your denunciation of the abuses of tobacco and wine. Yet, however sound in its principles, I expect it will be but a sermon to the wind. You will find it is as difficult to inculcate these sanative precepts on the sensualities of the present day as to convince an Athanasian[13] that there is but one God. I wish success to both attempts, and am happy to learn from you that the latter, at least, is making progress, and the more

rapidly in proportion as our Platonizing Christians make more stir and noise about it. The doctrines of Jesus are simple, and tend to the happiness of man:

1. That there is one only God, and He all perfect.
2. That there is a future state of rewards and punishments.
3. That to love God with all thy heart and thy neighbor as thyself, is the sum of religion.

These are the great points on which He endeavored to reform the religion of the Jews. But compare these with the demoralizing dogmas of Calvin:

1. That there are three Gods.
2. That good works, or the love of our neighbor, are nothing.
3. That faith is everything, and the more incomprehensible the proposition, the more merit in its faith.
4. That reason in religion is of unlawful use.
5. That God, from the beginning, elected certain individuals to be saved, and certain others to be damned; and that no crimes of the former can damn them; no virtues of the latter save.

Now, which of these is the true and charitable Christian? He who believes and acts on the simple doctrines of Jesus? Or the impious dogmatists, as Athanasius and Calvin? . . . They are mere usurpers of the Christian name, teaching a counter-religion. . . . I rejoice that in this blessed country of free inquiry and belief, which has surrendered its creed and conscience to neither kings nor priests, the genuine doctrine of one only God is reviving, and I trust that there is not a *young man* now living in the United States who will not die an Unitarian.[14]

Anti-Christian Deists agreed with other Deists as to what constitutes true religion, but they contrasted this true religion with Christianity. Few were as generous as Frederick II, "the Great" (1712–1786), who ruled Prussia 1740–1786. Frederick considered all revealed religions equally bogus and tolerated them equally. "All religions are equally good if the people who profess them are honest, and if the Turks and pagans come and are willing to populate the land, we would build mosques and temples.... In this country everyone must be saved after his own fashion.... But preachers must not forget tolerance, for no persecution by them will be allowed."[15]

The early biblical scholar Hermann Samuel Reimarus (1694–1786) wrote *The Aims of Jesus and His Disciples*[16] from an "eloquent hatred" of Christianity. According to Reimarus, Jesus had not the slightest intention of founding a new religion. He died by being in the wrong place at the wrong time, and his disciples, not wanting to go back to their old jobs, invented the idea of Jesus' resurrection.

In France, Voltaire (François-Marie Arouet; 1694–1778) worked not for a purified Christianity but to get rid of Christianity altogether:

> All sensible men, all honest men must hold the Christian religion in dread. The great name of Theist, which is not sufficiently revered, is the only name one should take. The only gospel that we ought to read is the great book of nature, written by the hand of God and sealed with his seal. The only religion that we ought to profess is the religion of worshiping God and being a good person. It is as impossible that this pure and eternal religion should produce evil as it is that Christian fanaticism should not produce it.[17]

Voltaire's opinions found an echo in America in the writings of Thomas Paine (1737–1809), especially *The Age of Reason* (1794–1795), in which he ridiculed revealed religion as full of superstition and bad faith.

Rationalism in all its stripes aimed at freeing religion from its bondage to dogma and Scripture. It therefore repudiated much of Christian tradition and gave a prominent role to the new philosophies—especially empiricism—that were emerging at this time. Early crticiques by William Law (1686–1761), George Berkeley (1685–1753), Joseph Butler (1692–1752),[18] and others could not stem the flood of new ideas, which came to powerful expression in the founding documents of the United States of America.

The Rise of Biblical Criticism

Prior to the period of rationalism ("the Enlightenment") biblical interpretation was done through theological lenses—often allegorical or typological[19]—even though a more historical approach can occasionally be documented in those earlier times.[20] Beginning in the late seventeenth century, however, new methods of interpreting the Bible emerged in Europe, often amid conflict and sharp controversy. Scholars who developed these methods were concerned to uncover both the historical milieu out of which the biblical texts emerged and also the meaning such writings might have had for the earliest groups of readers. Involved in such inquiries are questions of textual sources, authorship, date of writing, occasion for writing, the authors' points of view, and the use of the text in later stages of tradition. For the past three hundred years, academic biblical study has been dominated by such an approach, variously called higher criticism, biblical criticism, historical criticism, or the historical-critical method.

The list of pioneers of biblical criticism is long, and the process by which its methods and assumptions were developed is complex.[21] One pioneer, sometimes called the "founder of modern biblical criticism,"[22] was a French monk, Richard Simon (1638–1712). Stimulated in part by his desire to oppose the Protestant emphasis on "scripture alone," Simon, from 1682 until his death, published several monumental works on the Bible in which he claimed the right to study the Bible in the same way as he would study other ancient literature. He rejected the idea of verbal inspiration, denied that Moses wrote the Pentateuch, concluded that the titles attached to the New Testament gospels do not indicate their origin, and tried to determine the original setting for the writing of the New Testament books.

Simon's work was severely opposed by many, but it found a hearing among later scholars like Johann Salomo Semler (1725–1791), a pastor's son who grew up at Halle, Germany, with pietist influence but was influenced by rationalist scholars during his student years. The distinction Semler made between religion (the personal appropriation of revealed truth) and theology (intellectual reflection on religious truths) allowed him unrestricted use of critical analysis in his study of the Bible. His major work, on the "free investigation of the canon," was published between 1771 and 1775. Semler here drew a distinction between the word of God and Holy Scripture; the Bible contains parts that were meaningful only for the time in which they were written and no longer serve to lead to "moral improvement." Not all of the Bible is equally inspired or normative. Moreover, the question of the canon (the list of books to be accounted Scripture) is a purely historical question, because the canon merely represents the agreement of the early churches. Thus, Semler concluded, the Revelation of John has no "food for the soul" and cannot be ascribed to the author of John's gospel. Also, in what turned out to be historically influential, he insisted that there was in early Christianity a sharp distinction between Jewish Christianity, represented by Peter, and Gentile Christianity, represented by Paul, and that most New Testament documents could be assigned to either of these two wings.

In explaining why the Bible might contain material of various degrees of revelation, Semler articulated the "theory of accommodation," the idea that God "accommodates" revelation to human ignorance and weakness, adapting revelation to the limits of what the people of any given age could understand.[23] Revelation progresses in each subsequent age; anthropomorphisms and other crudities are left behind as one epoch leads to another. Semler's work introduced relativity into the concept of biblical authority, an issue that would be suppressed only with difficulty.

Meanwhile, the techniques of ancient Hebrew poetry—most of the Old Testament was written as poetry—were recovered by Robert Lowth of London (1710–1787) and Johann Gottfried von Herder in Germany (1744–180).

A host of scholarly giants was to follow in the nineteenth century and beyond, among them David Friedrich Strauss (1808–1874) and Ferdinand Christian Baur (1792–1860) on the New Testament side and Julius Wellhausen (1844–1918) and Hermann Gunkel (1862–1932) in the study of the Old Testament. Each of these left a powerful influence on biblical scholars to the present day.

Critical (analytical) and historical methods of interpreting the Bible are part of the rationalist movement within the Enlightenment, but such methods also belong to the "modern" worldview. Only in recent decades—during the rise of postmodernism—have there been serious challenges to the assumptions of the "historical critical method."

Conclusion

It sometimes seems that persons are genetically programmed to tend toward one or another of these three approaches to ultimate questions. Orthodoxism—and its less intellectual offspring, fundamentalism—offers ideological certainty and final answers to individuals who are uncomfortable with ambiguity and who seek a strong sense of personal and tribal identity. Pietism appeals to those for whom truth has a strong emotional component and for whom the changed heart is the answer to the evils of earthly life. And rationalism is followed by persons who recoil from tribal passions and the polemics of rival orthodoxies and who foster moral improvement and universal goodwill. The three emphasize thinking, feeling, and doing, respectively.[24]

11

COPERNICUS, DARWIN, AND FREUD
The Crisis of Modernist Worldviews

Methinks the Holy Ghost intends to teach us not how the heavens go but how to go to heaven.

> —Attributed, in various wordings, most often to Galileo but also
> to Cesare Baronius, Augustine, Pope John Paul II, and others[1]

The issue: How could Christianity adapt to modern changes in worldviews?

A series of ideological crises of the first magnitude spans the entire period from the Reformation until today. These crises can be summed up as the diminution of the human being in the great scheme of things. If during the Middle Ages and into the Reformation it was natural to believe that human beings occupied the center of the universe, standing apart from all other creatures as the unique object of God's concern, these beliefs changed with three great revolutions of thought. Nicolaus Copernicus described how human beings are situated in a corner of the universe, Charles Darwin put the development of the human being in a biological chain of cause and effect within the natural world, and Sigmund Freud sought a natural and rational explanation for the entire category of inner human life and what it means to be religious. Along with major developments in the natural sciences and industrial technology, these revolutions accompanied and reflected the optimistic attitude that humans can discover the essences of reality and harness them to foster the progressive advancement of the human race. Such was the worldview of the period of modernism.

The Copernican Revolution

Thales (ca. 600 B.C.E.) and Pythagoras (ca. 580–500 B.C.E.) were among the pre-Socratic Greeks who speculated that the earth was round. Plato (427–347 B.C.E.) observed that the earth casts a round shadow on the moon during a lunar eclipse; he concluded that the earth rotates on an axis. Aristarchus of Samos (third century B.C.E.) was convinced that the earth rotates, revolves around the sun, and is not at the center of the cosmos. And Eratosthenes (ca. 276–194 B.C.E.), by comparing noon sightings of the sun at the summer solstice from points five hundred miles apart, fairly accurately calculated the circumference of the earth.

The views and discoveries of the ancient Greeks, however, did not prevail, largely because of the enormous influence of Ptolemy (second century C.E.), who taught that the sun, moon, and planets revolve in solid, transparent spheres around the stationary earth. Beyond them is the sphere of the fixed stars, and beyond that is the Empyrean (heaven, paradise). Although this theory involved complex explanations of the orbits of the heavenly objects, in other respects it appealed to common sense: If the earth rotates, why don't clouds and objects on the surface fly off? And if you throw a ball straight up, why does it fall back down to the same point on the earth? And if the earth revolves around the sun, why do the stars always appear to be in the same relative position?

The Ptolemaic worldview prevailed among scholars until the Renaissance. Common people, however, thought that the earth was flat, with hell below and heaven above.

As many historians and theologians have pointed out, both Ptolemaic cosmology and the worldview of the common people of the Middle Ages presupposed the infinite significance of humanity, the purposiveness of everything, and the absolute necessity of the church and its sacraments. Hell and heaven were realistically imagined, and miracles were to be expected. Pilgrimages and relics were unexceptional. It was natural to believe that human salvation was God's main occupation.

A Polish monk, Nicolaus Copernicus (1473–1543), shattered the medieval worldview by propounding a detailed theory of heliocentricity. Already in 1531 in his *Commentariolus* (Little commentary) he summarized his views: The sun is at the center of the universe; around it revolve the planets, including the earth, which also rotates on fixed poles daily.

Copernicus's full theory, *De revolutionibus orbium coelestium* (On the revolution of the heavenly orbs) was published in 1543 with the aid of twenty-five-year-old Georg Rheticus, who was a Lutheran professor at Wittenberg and one of Melanchthon's students. Copernicus died within an hour of seeing one of the first copies.

The churches reacted negatively. Martin Luther called him a "fool" who should know that Joshua commanded the sun, not the earth, to stand still (a reference to Josh 10:12–13). John Calvin quoted Ps 93:1: The Lord "has established the world; it shall never be moved." And Pope Clement VII complained that Copernicus had the temerity to contradict Aristotle.

Heliocentricity was controversial because it seemed to be at odds with the claim that the Bible provides a scientifically accurate picture of the cosmos; it appeared to minimize the need for supernatural causes of earthly occurrences; and especially because it dethroned the human being to residence on a piece of cosmic dust floating in the backyard of an endless universe. By the time of Isaac Newton (1642–1727), however, the church had learned to live with the new worldview. But even Newton thought that the earth as it now is was created only a few thousand years ago.

The Darwinian Revolution

The idea of evolution was not invented by Charles Darwin. Some Greek philosophers thought along these lines, as did the philosopher G. F. W. Hegel (1770–1831; Hegel's interests, however, were much more abstruse than those of biologists). Toward the turn of the eighteenth century there was a growing interest in speculating about human and earthly origins. In 1799 the French astronomer and mathematician Pierre-Simon Laplace (1749–1827) published *Exposition of the System of the World,* and in his 1830 *Principles of Geology* British geologist Charles Lyell (1797–1875) argued that the present form of the universe was the result of an extremely long process.

Influenced by such predecessors, Charles Darwin (1809–1882) spent thirty years, some of them in far-flung places of the earth, collecting evidence to support his theory that life had evolved by a process of natural selection. Darwin was impressed by the great variety of living organisms, and he was aware of such things as the relationships of fossils found in different strata of the earth. His findings were published in his epoch-making book *The Origin of the Species by Means of Natural Selection,* or the *Preservation of Favored Races in the Struggle for Life* (1859).

The Origin of the Species has two basic theses: (1) The species of plants and animals are not fixed and immutable from the hand of the Creator, but from certain individuals within the species the species itself changes to form a new, usually more complex species. All species evolved from a few—or perhaps one—species. (2) This whole process is governed by a simple law, namely, natural selection. Those individuals and species best adapted to their environment survive and the others become extinct. By nature cautious, Darwin used evidence from plants and some animals but mentioned the origin of humans only once in the entire book: "Light will be thrown on the origin of man and his history." But the implications were obvious: the earth is extremely old and has been populated by many kinds of animals and plants, many of whom are no longer living. The human race—also mutable—originated long ago as well.

Within one year Darwin's book was the most talked-about book in Europe. Its effect in America was delayed by the Civil War, but within ten years of that war almost all important scientists in Europe and America had been converted to Darwin's theories. Moreover, scholars beyond the sciences were beginning to adopt the evolutionary approach.

In his *Zoological Evidences as to Man's Place in Nature* (1863), Thomas H. Huxley (1825–1895) suggested on the basis of anatomical comparisons that human evolution had taken place in much the same way as that of apes. Darwin entered the fray in 1871 with *The Descent of Man,* allowing for the possibility that apes and humans have the same ancestor. Many persons, however, misunderstood Darwin and Huxley to say that human beings are descended from apes as the species of apes is today. Bishop Samuel Wilberforce (1805–1873) of Oxford and Winchester reportedly responded, "How can high-class turnips become men?"

The churches generally reacted negatively and vehemently, presumably because the theory reduced the role of the Creator to a minimum (and excluded the idea of creation out of nothing) and minimized the boundary between human beings and other animals. This reductionism involved the object of Christian devotion (the first case) and the possibility of Christian ethics (the second case). Natural selection, "nature red in tooth and claw," was hardly a moral concept. The traditional orthodoxists and biblical authoritarians agreed with Charles Hodge (1797–1878) of Princeton Seminary: "A more absolutely incredible theory was never propounded for acceptance among men."[2] Hodge's positions on the Bible and evolution are similar to those of early twentieth-century fundamentalists as seen in the Scopes trial of 1925, in which John T. Scopes (1900–1970) was accused of teaching evolution in the public schools of Dayton, Tennessee, violating the law against teaching evolution.

The Roman Catholic Church responded more deliberately. In 1950 Pope Pius XII promulgated the bull *Humani generis* (Human origins), which rejected any statement that excluded the Creator, while allowing evolution with respect to the body but not the soul.

The uniqueness of human beings could thereby be preserved, but on the basis of a rather artificial distinction between body and soul.

Some Christians saw in Darwin's theory new evidence of God's method in creation, and gradually all came to realize that both the church and Darwin are here to stay. It would no longer be easily possible, however, to maintain the qualitative uniqueness of human beings in relation to the animal world. Christian theology again faced the challenge of relativism.

The Freudian Revolution

The work of the Viennese neurologist Sigmund Freud (1856–1939) confronted Christian theology with perhaps even greater challenges than did that of Copernicus or Darwin. Psychoanalytic theory and practice not only offered a nonreligious description of the inner life of human beings but also could function as a rival system of salvation (wholeness)—without guilt, without forgiveness, and without God.

Basic to psychoanalytic theory are the concepts of the subconscious and repression. Only a fraction of our mental activity is conscious. One avenue to our subconcious, a rather subjective one, is the state of dreaming. Human beings are driven by elementary instinctual impulses aimed at satisfying primal needs, one of the strongest of which is sex. Many of our problems stem from the repression of such instinctual drives by familial and societal structures. Although repressed, these drives are not dormant; they seek expression in one way or another.

Freud gradually became convinced that two basic tendencies are connected with sexuality. Alongside of eros, the creative and supporting drive, there is the death instinct, which is bent on returning the individuals to their primordial, inorganic condition and which is exhibited most typically in aggression. Freud sought to explain the phenomena of life by the interchange of these two drives: "The battle between eros and death, between the drives toward life and destruction, is, according to Freud, the essential content of life and is indicative of human struggle for survival."[3]

In the human psyche, according to Freud, three functions or components can be distinguished. The id consists of chaotic and unconscious drives, predominantly libido, the impulse to reproduce. The id is bound to bodily functions, progressing from the oral phase of nursing through the anal phase to the genital or Oedipal phase, which for males is characterized by the death wish against the father and an incest wish toward the mother. The ego, by contrast, is oriented toward the external world, mediating external stimuli toward the id. The superego has its origin in the internalizing of outside authority as a socializing function (the laws and mores of society are in reality a collective superego). But the superego can drive a person to neurosis, melancholy, guilt, aggression, and even suicide.

In a long series of books and essays, Freud articulated his conviction that mental illness could be cured by self-knowledge gained by psychoanalysis. Becoming aware of repressed drives of the unconscious can lead to wholeness. Freud was convinced that religious experience often originated from the projection of individual inner conflicts. Psychoanalysis could function as a worldview in itself.[4] Although Freudianism in many circles has lost its sheen in the face of biological and chemical explanations of neuroses and psychoses, the relativizing of religious ideas and the naturalistic explanation of religious experience that it fostered has retained its force.

The Ecumenical Movement as a Symptom of Modernism

The optimistic assumptions about technological and scientific progress, human perfectability, and the upward push of evolution that characterized the modernist period are in some ways similar to the thinking and motivations behind the emergence of the ecumenical movement that emerged just after the turn of the twentieth century. Prior to the world wars, many church leaders hoped and believed that the centuries-long divisions of Western Christianity might be overcome and that the twentieth century would be the "Christian century," marked by the rapid spread of the church throughout the world. Thus a comment on the ecumenical movement may rightfully be included in this chapter on the modernist period.

As demonstrated in the preceding chapters of this book, Christendom has never in fact been united. Tensions in the earliest church between Hellenistic Jewish Christians and Palestinian Jewish Christians are evident in the book of Acts. Dissident groups emerged within the first generation of Christians, and the history of the church can be understood as one of recurring dissension and conflict. Some of the schisms had permanent effects (for example, the Nestorians, the Great Schism of 1054, the European Reformation), while numerous other dissident groups disappeared.

The ecumenical movement of the modern period aims, in various ways and with different strategies, at bringing greater unity to a fragmented Christendom. Ecumenists argue that there already is unity in some respects; Christians have much in common, whatever their institutional differences. The goal is understood variously.[5] A few hope for complete organic unity, with all Christians united in one earthly organization. Others aim at universal mutual recognition of all Christians, with full sharing of the Eucharist and ministry. Still others are content at the initial stage to work for increased cooperation in areas of mutual concern on the part of various denominations in a federation of churches.

The first half of the twentieth century saw the move toward church unity on several fronts:

- Numerous mergers within church families occurred, especially in the United States, where, for example, Lutheran churches that had a separate European national and linguistic background came together.
- International alliances of denominations of the same family, such as the World Alliance of Reformed and Presbyterian Churches and the Lutheran World Federation, were created.
- National councils of churches (for example, the National Council of the Churches of Christ in the United States) came into being.
- International, interdenominational cooperation was put into practice.

The most active ecumenical institution of the third kind is certainly the World Council of Churches.[6] Its roots go back to a conference of several Christian missionary societies at Edinburgh in 1910. Three concerns were identified: the missionary task of the church, the common service the churches could render to the world, and doctrinal disagreements responsible for ongoing division. To deal with the first concern, the International Missionary Council was established in 1921. To address the second concern, the Commission on Life and Work held its first meeting in Stockholm in 1925. And the third concern resulted in the establishment of Faith and Order, which met initially in 1927 in Lausanne. Further ecumenical work was delayed by the horrors of World War II. Then, in Amsterdam in 1948, delegates from some 146 churches—Protestant, Anglican, and Orthodox—created the World Council of Churches (WCC) by merging Life and Work with Faith and Order. Finally, the International Missionary Council joined the WCC in 1961.

The increasing fragmentation of Western society in the latter half of the twentieth century, however, abruptly inaugurated a postmodern mentality and thereby also seriously dimmed the earlier fervor for institutional church unity. G. R. Evans begins her assessment of the current status of ecumenism with an introduction titled "The Winter of Ecumenism":

> In the late 1960s it began to look as though it would be possible to achieve within our lifetime a definitive coming together in unity between a number of the existing separated communions. . . . But in many cases the churches which joined in this enterprise so eagerly at first are not proving able to make wholeheartedly their own the agreements arrived at through the dialogues; and consequently they cannot act out such agreements in actually moving towards union.[7]

Conclusion

Copernicus, Darwin, and Freud are typical of the multitude of scholars who accomplished the permanent shattering of the ancient and medieval worldviews with which Christianity had become comfortable. They represent full-blown modernity—the self-assured attitude that the physical universe, human biological history, and the human psyche itself along with its intellectual creations can be explained scientifically by rational experimentation and reflection. In the twentieth century, however, modernity itself would be relativized.

Modernism was a red flag for many conservative Christians in North America in the early decades of the twentieth century. The attempt by such popular American preachers and teachers as Walter Rauschenbusch and Harry Emerson Fosdick to find an honest and intellectually viable modus vivendi with the new sciences and technology seemed to such critics to concede overly much to science and secularism. In an ironic twist of fate, many conservative Christians at the end of the twentieth century found themselves battling postmodern fragmentation and arguing on the basis of positivist assumptions that were more typical of the modern period.

12

THE CHALLENGE TO CHRISTIAN FAITH TODAY
The Crisis of Postmodernism

"Christendom" is . . . the betrayal of Christianity.

—Soren Kierkegaard[1]

The thing that keeps coming back to me is, what is Christianity, and indeed what is Christ, for us today? . . . We are proceeding towards a time of no religion at all. . . . Those who honestly describe themselves as "religious" do not in the least act up to it, and so when they say "religious" they evidently mean something quite different. . . . If we had to put down the western pattern of Christianity as a mere preliminary stage to doing without religion altogether, what situation would result for us, for the Church? How can Christ become the Lord even of those with no religion? If religion is no more than the garment of Christianity—and even that garment has had very different aspects at different periods, then what is a religionless Christianity?

—Dietrich Bonhoeffer, April 30, 1944[2]

The issue: How should Christians and Christian theology respond to postmodern ambiguity?

Generalizations about the present are by their nature subject to change or even reversal. Many perceptive observers, however, are convinced that there is a common cultural mood in the West in the early third millennium, and that it differs markedly from what prevailed two hundred or even one hundred and fifty years ago. Because this sense of change comes after the optimistic rational certainty of the modern period, it is often labeled postmodernity.[3] Central to the postmodern atmosphere is the feeling that the medieval and modern synthesis of meaning has collapsed, and we have no universally trusted sets of symbols by which to live. What was taken as given in an earlier age is no longer so, and we have no choice but to live with ambiguity, relativism, subjectivity, and contingency. The universal has given way to the contextual, the general to the local, and hegemonic thinking to pluralism. In postmodernism there can be no universal truth or general system but only a set of competing claims and narratives.

Antecedents

During the nineteenth century new and unfamiliar voices were beginning to be heard in European intellectual circles. In some cases the impact of these new voices would not be felt in full power until the latter half of the twentieth century. Among these voices are two fascinating and prolific writers of great passion who analyzed human existence and drew from this analysis weighty conclusions about Christianity and what it means to live a fully human life. Søren Kierkegaard, a founder of existentialism, was a thoroughly convinced Christian, while Friedrich Nietzsche announced the passing of the Christian epoch and the hope for the emergence of the *Übermensch,* the new self-confident and just human being who needs no ideology and no god. Both figures, however, anticipate the postmodern rejection of moral absolutes and eternal verities.

Søren Kierkegaard (1813–1855)

Søren Kierkegaard, Denmark's most significant theologian and philosopher, was a brilliant loner of acute personal and spiritual sensibility. Several of his religious and devotional writings have become classics, among them *Fear and Trembling*, an analysis from several angles of Abraham's near sacrifice of Isaac; *Purity of Heart*; *Sickness unto Death*; *For Self-Examination*; and *The Concept of Dread*. Toward the end of his life he wrote increasingly bitter and sarcastic tracts on the Church of Denmark and on "Christendom" in general; some of these are published as *Attack upon Christendom*.

Kierkegaard's analysis of the basic modes of human existence was developed in his first book, *Either-Or* (1843).[4] In this work, he argues that there are three ever-present possibilities for the individual human being.

The esthetic life is expressed variably as sensual immediacy (Don Juan), doubt (Faust), or despair (Ahasuerus, the Wandering Jew). The esthete lacks moral will and drifts along in the search for the pleasurable moment, which can never be satisfied. Despair, however, can lead either to death or to awakening that leads to salvation.

The ethical mode involves absolute choice—passionate, uncondi-tional choice—and a commitment to know and *to become* the truth. Ethical decision gives a person a sense of inner coherence. But moral theology such as that of Immanuel Kant trivializes human sin and guilt and ignores the human need for grace.

The religious mode offers two possibilities: "Religiousness A," the religion of Socrates, and "Religiousness B," the religion of Jesus Christ. Kierkegaard developed the distinction between the two reli-gious options in *Philosophical Fragments* (1844). Religiousness A is based on the assumption that, as taught by Plato and Socrates, Truth is latent within every human being. In this case what is needed is a midwife to enable a person to give birth to the Truth that lies within, to stimulate recollection of true knowledge. Here the slogan is "Know thyself": that is, recollect the Truth that is latent within you.

If, however, Socrates was wrong and humans of themselves live in Error, then Truth must be *acquired*. The teacher must not only bring the Truth but also provide the condition (awareness of being in Error) for the hearer to understand it. Such a teacher should be called Savior and Redeemer and must come to human beings from the outside. To accomplish this, God must descend and appear before humankind in real history—not in glory but as a servant. The Incarnation of the Eternal in time surpasses all human comprehension. It is the "Absolute Paradox," "the Miracle," "the Absurd," for it claims that the Eternal has become temporal and that eternal happiness depends on a historical event. Kierkegaard's thought is thus unmistakably incarnational. Among his most famous utterances is the following: "If the contemporary generation had left nothing behind them but these words: 'We have believed that in such and such a year God appeared among us in the humble figure of a servant, that he lived and taught in our community, and finally died,' it would be more than enough."[5]

When Kierkegaard asserted that "Truth is subjectivity," he separated other kinds of knowledge from religious experience, which involves personal appropriation and cannot be reduced to dogmatic systems. Kierkegaard sought in brilliant and sometimes infuriating ways to "divorce Christianity from a complacent, bourgeois culture" and to direct human beings "to the infinite qualitative difference between the transcendent, unknowable God, and finite, sinful" human beings.[6] For him there was no proof of Christianity, no convincing apologetic apart from divine revelation. Salvation can come only from the wholly other. In all this, Kierkegaard demolished rational and liberal Christian theology and functioned as a decisive influence not only on the "existentialist" philosophers and theologians but especially on the greatest of twentieth-century theologians, Karl Barth (1886–1968).

Friedrich Nietzsche (1844–1900)

The son of a German Lutheran pastor, Friedrich Nietzsche was heavily influenced by the atheism and emphasis on the will, rather than reason, of Arthur Schopenhauer's *World as Will and Idea* (1818). Nietzsche's attitude toward Christianity was expressed in such works as *The Gay Science* (1882), *Thus Spake Zarathustra* (1883–1891), *Beyond Good and Evil* (1886), *A Genealogy of Morals* (1887), and *The Antichrist* (1888).[7]

Nietzsche saw the modern world as in a state of cultural nihilism, in which human rationality—including all theology and all metaphysics—had run its course and society was dominated by crude materialism. Nietzsche observed as a cultural fact that most educated persons of his time were practical atheists—God was no longer the integral center or even a part of their lives. This "death of God" is announced both by a madman in the streets[8] and the prophet Zarathustra (Zoroaster) descending a mountain. The death of God, neither the fact nor the consequences of which are fully perceived as yet, implies the end of traditional values and the loss of the grounding of life. To continue to believe in God is to embrace nihilism and to live in a world of fiction; but to live without God is to strip everything of meaning and value.

Nietzsche believed that Christianity itself contained within it the seeds of the death of God. Christian belief and practice are the unconscious products of resentment of the weak masses against their aristocratic superiors. This resentment is part of the universal human will to power, a form of "slave morality" in distinction from the aristocratic "master morality." "Slave morality" inverts aristocratic values such as good/noble/powerful/beautiful/happy (as with the ancient Greeks) to foster love and the blessing of the poor, the powerless, and the sick. Jesus and the Christian church universalized the existing Jewish "transvaluation of values."

Jesus, according to Nietzsche, represented childlike qualities, a sense of blessedness and freedom from the cares of the world that was not shaken even by the sufferings that led to his death. Even so, his passivity would lead to nihilism. But, says Nietzsche, the apostle Paul transformed the gospel into a doctrine of revenge and decadence by inventing his own Christianity with the doctrine of justification by faith. This doctrine became the substitute both for action and for reason—a sacrifice of the intellect. Christianity thus exhibits a weakness that promotes contempt for all honest values.

What is needed is a new type of human existence—the *Übermensch* (superior human), who will be the successor of God. The *Übermensch* will have achieved self-mastery, self-discipline, abundance, joy, and natural grace in fulfillment of duty.

Nietzsche shares with Kierkegaard not only a harshly critical stance vis-à-vis Western culture but also a poetic and compelling analysis of human finitude. But, while Kierkegaard believed that the solution was to restore the heart of Christian faith and experience, Nietzsche found hope in a coming post-Christian world.

Competing Voices

Postmodernity involves a cacophony of voices clamoring to be heard, each claiming legitimacy. Among these voices are perspectives and approaches developed in the twentieth century that reflect different ideologies, ethnic groups, and genders as well as many who continue to locate themselves within traditional European thought. Examples of such variety within the circle of Christian theology abound.

Classical Protestant liberalism, like modernism in general, emphasized a positive image of humanity and held to the ideal of progress both with respect to technology, science, art, and even human perfectibility. Liberals located the center of Christian faith and life in the area of values, morality, and social ethics. They correspondingly depicted Jesus as a teacher of higher morality—the equality and dignity of all human beings before the gracious God.[9] Jesus' proclamation of the kingdom of God could be understood in liberalism as the end of an evolutionary process. The American Social Gospel movement, associated with Walter Rauschenbusch (1861–1918), can be understood as a specific form of Protestant liberalism. The movement in general suffered a severe shock at the horrors of the First World War.

Fundamentalism, a rather nontheological, American form of orthodoxism that flourished in the years following the First World War, held to the literal inerrancy of the Bible in all its parts and to a short list of other doctrines, including the divinity of Christ, his vicarious suffering for human sin, and his bodily return to earth at the end time.

American evangelicalism, which has flourished after Second World War up to the present, has perhaps more in common with pietism than orthodoxism and is often involved with social issues and with academic theology. One offshoot of evangelicalism is the

"Christian coalition" that has gained significant political influence in the United States, largely by emphasizing issues related to sexual morality.

Neoorthodoxy, as represented especially by Karl Barth (1886–1968),[10] is a strongly negative reaction to all forms of theological liberalism, especially natural theology and historical-critical approaches to the Bible. Barth, in some ways reminiscent of John Calvin, affirmed the utter transcendence of God to the extent that human reason is not only hopelessly useless in matters of faith but actually sinful. Apart from divine revelation, there is no knowledge of God of any kind to be had. True faith can learn nothing from the quest of the historical Jesus, because God is revealed in Jesus as the Christ only in an event that breaks the bounds of history, namely, his resurrection. In Jesus as the risen Christ all humanity is taken up and sin and evil are shown to be nothingness.

Feminist theology as it has developed over the past fifty years, especially in North America, has raised crucial questions not adequately dealt with in prior Christian theology: Is the human and religious experience of women qualitatively different from that of men? Can women participate fully in the use of masculine language and imagery for God? Has such imagery led in the past to hierarchical thought and to relegating women to a position of inferiority? Can women relate to Christian atonement theories that explain the death of Jesus as a vicarious sacrifice or as the placating of a wrathful God or as the "satisfaction" of an insult? Can women find true personhood and at the same time practice Christian ideals of sacrifice and humility? Creative work on these questions continues unabated.[11]

Liberation theology began as an attempt to apply Christian theology to societal reform in Latin America. It centers on the conviction that sin is basically a social, historical fact—alienation from others and from God. Sin can be seen in the structures of oppression, the exploitation of classes of people, and the conquest and enslavement of races and nations. Symptoms of sin include poverty, injustice, and oppression. As such, sin requires liberation, which has already been procured by virtue of the death and resurrection of Jesus.[12]

Black theology and womanist theology can be viewed as variants of liberation theology and feminist theology that deal more explicitly with issues that characterize the experience of African Americans.

New methods of literary criticism, including structuralism, reader-response criticism, narrative criticism, and several other approaches, have made it abundantly clear that the interpretation of texts—including the Bible—is a much more subjective enterprise than was thought to be the case in the modern epoch. Because interpretation must necessarily take place in the mind of the reader, it can never be possible to arrive fully at the original meaning of a text or the meaning for its first readers or the intention of the author. According to most contemporary literary critics, there is no one legitimate interpretation. Whether it is possible to assign degrees of legitimacy to various interpretations, however, remains in dispute.

Postmodernism, in short, implies that there is no universal truth but only competing sets of meaning or narratives. Can Christian theology find its way in this sea of relativity?

Postmodernity and Christian Theology

Christian scholars are beginning to suggest ways for biblical interpretation and theology to be done with integrity in a postmodern culture. In a number of books Walter Brueggemann has suggested that biblical interpretation center on attending to the "transformative imagination" of biblical texts.[13] According to Brueggemann, what the church needs in a postmodern milieu is a vision that can point beyond the prevailing despair of a consumer society—a counter-imagination. By means of a careful remembering of the past and creative imagining of the future, we can gain a transforming sense of the self, the world, and our community. Such biblical reading can be evocative of newness by opening for us vistas beyond our world of competitive consumerism, revealing a world in which human dignity takes precedence over profit and hope prevails over despair.

Transformative biblical reading such as Brueggemann proposes can be done by careful consideration of one manageable text at a time without the trappings of scholarly apparatus. In this enterprise

rhetorical sensitivity and reading with self-awareness become cru-
cially important. The reader or listener is called to participate by
considering alternate groups of metaphors and allusions that subver-
sively enable us to examine our old world at the same time as new
models of reality take shape before us. Engagement with the texts,
therefore, can lead to genuine *metanoia,* which can be translated better as "mind-change" than "repentance."

With regard to Christian systematic theology, Douglas John Hall
has analyzed the positivist mentality that was dominant in North
American culture up to about the middle of the twentieth century
and the crisis that has resulted from its decline. In the classic *Lighten
Our Darkness,* first published in 1976,[14] he described the hallmarks
of the typical *American expectation:* optimism, rationality, progress,
human perfectibility, domination of nature, denial of unpleasant-
ness, and dread of failure. When mixed with elements of Christian
belief, such hopes and assumptions amounted to a "theology of glory" tied up with the feeling of Christian entitlement that could be
traced back to the Constantinian settlement of the fourth century.
The converse was equally powerful: unreflective optimism about
human potential led to Western Christian shame regarding the traditional Christian association with the darkness of human life—with
sin, death, and the devil—and with the meaninglessness, loneliness,
injustice, guilt, and shame that real human beings experience.

Hall describes the Constantinian establishment as the creation of
"Christendom,"[15] the radical decline of which we in the West now
experience even as we try to warm ourselves by its embers. Can
Christian theology in the third millennium survive in a postmodern,
post-Christendom context?

To regain the authenticity of the Christian voice in North America,
Hall in his entire corpus insists that we give attention to a profound
minority strand in Christian history that runs from Paul to Luther to
Kierkegaard to Barth. This "thin tradition," so at odds with Western
culture, is the theology of the cross, the foundational belief that God
shared the sorrow and suffering of humankind and came among us
to keep hope alive in the midst of grippingly real darkness.[16] The theology of the cross calls Christians away from the search for political

and cultural hegemony, a search that can lead only to spiritual malaise and false hope, and to the path that can bring healing and wholeness to a broken world.

John Milbank of Cambridge University and his colleagues seek a way for Christian thought to remain credible and potent in the postmodern context.[17] They intend to establish the cogency of a theological "radical orthodoxy" in the context of our postmodern "soulless, aggressive, nonchalant, and nihilistic" secular materialism.[18] Secular nihilism, in fact, is seen as "an ontology of power and conflict which is simply another *mythos,* a kind of re-invented paganism."[19] Instead of rejecting the hallmarks of postmodernism, however, Milbank and his colleagues attempt to show that the "sites" in which modern and postmodern secularism have heavily invested—aesthetics, politics, sex, the body, personhood, visibility, and space—can be more compellingly situated within traditional Christian categories such as Trinity, Christology, church, and Eucharist. This approach is "orthodox" in its allegiance to creedal Christianity, its engagement with the church fathers, and its efforts to recover a "fully Christianized ontology and practical philosophy."[20] It is radical in the sense of returning to patristic and medieval roots, in its systematic critique of contemporary society and culture, its rethinking of Christian tradition, and its insistence on a more incarnate, participatory, aesthetic, erotic, and "Platonic" Christianity.

Conclusion

Postmodernism's insistence on the relativity and subjectivity of truth constitutes a crisis for Christianity in the twenty-first century. Most Western Christians have the sense that, despite the resurgence of more fundamentalist forms of the faith in recent decades, the era of Christendom is coming to an end. Such radical change is not easy; it is often accompanied by anxiety. Change, however, is seldom all bad, and the resilience of the faith over the centuries suggests that—along with secularism—it will endure to face new crises in the centuries to come.

EPILOGUE
Crisis and Meaning

The significance of Christianity for world history, according to Hegel, is the public record of its historical development. Christianity is meaningful because of its impact on historical existence as such. It reveals the purpose of human existence at a crucial stage of humanity's cultural evolution. A scholarly and philosophical account of Christian history is the proper defense of religion and the path to truth.

—Roy A. Harrisville and Walter Sundberg,
The Bible in Modern Culture[1]

Followers of Jesus from the beginning up to the present have hoped and prayed for unity among themselves. But this ideal has never been realized. The New Testament Gospels trace disputes among the original disciples back to the time of Jesus' activity in Galilee. It is true that a core set of beliefs—for example, God's exaltation of Jesus after his death—can be found among all early Christians. Nonetheless, a fascinating variety of belief and practice has characterized the Christian movement from the conflicts reflected in Paul's letters and the book of Acts down through the subsequent centuries. Indeed, it is not difficult to find in the early and medieval churches parallels to almost every variety of Christianity in our fragmented world today. Recognizing the diversity in two millennia of Christian belief and thought, we can more easily celebrate variety in faith and practice today and welcome those whose piety differs from ours.

Conflicts among Christians, some of them convulsive, have at times hampered the movement or limited its growth, as can be seen most glaringly in the ancient doctrinal controversies, the Great Schism between the Eastern and Western churches in 1054, and the Protestant Reformations of the sixteenth century. But such profound disagreements also have often had a creative effect, functioning as the catalyst for the development of both doctrine and practice. An understanding of these conflicts opens the door to new perspectives from which to appreciate the various components of the church's tradition—its creeds and structures as well as its veneration of the early writings that make up the New Testament.

The idea that Christian doctrine and practice evolve by means of a largely natural process of conflict raises the question of the nature and function of theology and its relation to the question of truth. This issue is clarified when we recognize that the function of Christian theology is not to put into words timeless truths once revealed or dogmatic propositions valid for all generations. Theology (literally, "a word about God") has two functions, both of which are driven by context.

First, theology has the function of systematizing core Christian beliefs, putting them into a consistent framework of thought and supplying for them a rationale. The value of this task is to assist Christians in the process of self-understanding, of conceptualizing what they profess to believe.

Theology has the important second function of presenting Christian belief in a credible and intelligible form to the broader society. This task, traditionally known as apologetics (from the Greek *apologia*, "defense"), obviously takes into account the prevailing intellectual, philosophical, and general cultural assumptions of the time. Thus, for example, Origen used the basic categories of Platonism to express the Christian beliefs that he inherited, Tertullian used categories of Latin legal traditions to coin a new theological vocabulary, and several theologians of the twentieth century were able to convey theology in terms of existential thought framed by Søren Kierkegaard and others. In the beginning of the third millennium, several theologians are concerned with expressing Christian belief in terms of the postmodernism that has been developed by literary critics and philosophers. Core Christian beliefs persist through the ages, but the understanding of them and the systematizing of them must necessarily be done in the dominant categories of thought of the age.

If theology is driven by context, does it have a timeless subject matter, that is, raw material? During the second century Christian writers spoke of the *regula fidei* (rule of faith) or the "canon of truth," beliefs they considered to be universally held by all Christians and unchanged from the beginning of the church.[2] And some theologians today refer to "normative Christianity," by which they mean a trajectory of belief that, they argue, formed the starting point for Christian theology from the time of the apostles to our own age.[3] These concepts appear to be incipient creedal statements and usually include convictions that resemble the Apostles' Creed: monotheism, creation, Jesus' redemptive death and resurrection, the possibility of human redemption, and the hope for eternal life. Oddly enough, the content of what Jesus himself *taught* is usually not a major component of such lists. In itself, the *regula fidei* does not show *how* Jesus' life, death, and resurrection are redemptive; it only insists on the necessity to believe that they are. The theologian's task, then, is to create a system of thought in which these inherited beliefs are related in a consistent and understandable way. Academic theology, then, is perhaps more a fascinating diversion than a necessity for most Christians, even though it is a significant and necessary task for Christianity as such.

For Further Reading

Adam, A. K. M., ed. *Handbook of Postmodern Biblical Interpretation*. St. Louis: Chalice Press, 2000.

Bainton, Roland H. *The Age of the Reformation*. Princeton, N.J.: Van Nostrand, 1956.

———. *Early Christianity*. Princeton, N.J.: Van Nostrand, 1960.

———. *The Medieval Church*. Princeton, N.J.: Van Nostrand, 1962.

Balling, Jakob. *The Story of Christianity from Birth to Global Presence*. Translated by the author. Grand Rapids, Mich.: Eerdmans, 2003.

Deanesly, Margaret. *A History of the Medieval Church, 590–1500*. 8th ed. London: Methuen, 1954. This classic remains fascinating and informative.

Dowley, Tim. *Introduction to the History of Christianity*. Minneapolis: Fortress Press, 1996. Graphically interesting presentation, with charts, maps, insets, and much helpful information.

Evans, Gillian R. *Method in Ecumenical Theology: The Lessons So Far*. Cambridge: Cambridge University Press, 1996.

Fahey, Michael A. *Ecumenism: A Bibliographical Overview*. Westport, Conn.: Greenwood Press, 1992. Exhaustive annotated bibliography.

Gonzalez, Justo L. *The Story of Christianity.* 2 vols. San Francisco: Harper, 1984–1985.

Lakeland, Paul. *Postmodernity: Christian Identity in a Fragmented Age.* Guides to Theological Inquiry. Minneapolis: Fortress Press, 1997.

Linwood, Urban. *A Short History of Christian Thought.* Rev. ed. New York: Oxford University Press, 1995.

Livingston, James C. *Modern Christian Thought.* Rev. ed. 2 vols. New York: Macmillan, 1997, 2000.

Marty, Martin E. *A Short History of Christianity.* Philadelphia: Fortress Press, 1987.

McManners, John. *The Oxford Illustrated History of Christianity.* Oxford and New York: Oxford University Press, 1990. Handsomely produced survey.

Meyer, Harding. *That All May Be One: Perceptions and Models of Ecumenicity.* Translated by William G. Rusch. Grand Rapids, Mich.: Eerdmans, 1999. The history of and approach to ecumenism on the part of various Christian traditions.

Pelikan, Jaroslav. *The Christian Tradition.* 5 vols. Chicago: University of Chicago Press, 1971–1989. Indispensable for the serious student of the history of Christian thought: *The Emergence of the Catholic Tradition* (100–600), 1971; *The Spirit of Eastern Christendom* (600–1700), 1974; *The Growth of Medieval Theology* (600–1300), 1978; *Reformation of Church and Dogma* (1300–1700), 1983; *Christian Doctrine and Modern Culture* (since 1700), 1989.

Placher, William C. *A History of Christian Theology: An Introduction.* Philadelphia: Westminster Press, 1983.

———. *Readings in the History of Christian Theology.* Philadelphia, Westminster Press, 1988.

Stark, Rodney. *The Rise of Christianity: A Sociologist Reconsiders History.* Princeton, N.J.: Princeton University Press, 1996.

Tillich, Paul. *A History of Christian Thought.* Edited by Carl Braaten. New York: Harper & Row, 1968. The great theologian's lectures during the height of his career at Union Seminary, New York, offer a creative, if idiosyncratic, look at the subject.

Voltaire (François Marie Arouet). *The Portable Voltaire*. Edited by Ben Ray Redman. New York: Viking, 1949.

Volz, Carl A. *The Medieval Church: From the Dawn of the Middle Ages to the Eve of the Reformation*. Nashville: Abingdon Press, 1997.

Walker, Williston, Richard A. Norris, David W. Lotz, and Robert T. Handy. *A History of the Christian Church*. 4th ed. New York: Scribner, 1985. A standard for several decades, updated periodically.

Notes

Preface

1. Paul R. Spickard and Kevin M. Cragg, in *A Global History of Christianity* (Grand Rapids, Mich.: Baker, 1994), include accounts of "everyday believers" and major figures and events in Christianity, both Western and worldwide.

Introduction

1. Simone de Beauvoir, *The Coming of Age* (trans. P. O'Brian; New York: Putnam, 1972), 373–438.

2. Vincent of Lérins, "A Commonitory," in *Nicene and Post-Nicene Fathers of the Christian Church* (ed. P. Schaff, et al.; Grand Rapids, Mich.: Eerdmans, 1955), 11:132.

Chapter 1

1. Adapted from the translation by James A. Kleist, *The Didache, The Epistle of Barnabas, The Epistles and Martyrdom of Polycarp, The Fragments of Papias, The Epistle to Diognetus* (Ancient Christian Writers 6; Westminster, Md.: The Newman Press, 1957), 21.

2. See Luke Timothy Johnson, *The Writings of the New Testament* (rev. ed.; Minneapolis: Fortress Press, 1999), 107–19.

3. According to the historian Josephus, *Jewish Antiquities* 20.9.1, and the Christian historian Eusebius, *The History of the Church* (trans. G. A. Williamson; Baltimore: Penguin, 1965), 4.23.4.

4. Eusebius, *History* 3.32.3–6.

5. See Hans-Joachim Schoeps, *Jewish Christianity* (trans. Douglas R. A. Hare; Philadelphia: Fortress Press, 1969).

6. The complexities in the study of the work and person of the apostle Paul are too great to be taken up here in any detail.

7. Several translations of the apostolic fathers are available. Excerpts quoted here are from the Loeb Library, which includes the Greek text along with an English translation by Kirsopp Lake in two volumes (Cambridge, Mass.: Harvard University Press, 1912–13), or from the series Ancient Christian Writers, translations of texts by James A. Kleist (see chap. 1, n. 1).

8. My emphasis.

9. *Martyrdom of Polycarp* 8.1.

10. *Epistle of Barnabas* 5.7.

11. *Epistle to Diognetus* 1.

12. See Rom 15:4; 1 Cor 10:11. This claim is explicit in numerous quotations of Old Testament passages, for example, in Matt 1–2, the passion narratives of the Gospels, Paul's letters, the Letter to the Hebrews, and elsewhere.

Chapter 2

1. Origen, *On First Principles* (trans. G. W. Butterworth; New York: Harper & Row, 1966), 1.

2. The classic argument against the idea is Walter Bauer, *Orthodoxy and Heresy in Earliest Christianity* (trans. R. A. Kraft; G. Krodel, et. al.; Philadelphia: Fortress Press, 1971). For a survey of the treatment of the question and a proposal different from Bauer's, see Arland J. Hultgren, *The Rise of Normative Christianity* (Minneapolis: Fortress Press, 1994).

3. A convenient collection of ancient anti-heretical sources is Arland J. Hultgren and Steven A. Haggmark, eds., *The Earliest Christian Heretics: Readings from Their Opponents* (Minneapolis: Fortress Press, 1996).

4. Apollinarius, bishop of Hierapolis in the latter half of the second century; his account cited here is from the extensive quotation by Eusebius, *History* 5.16.

5. In 2001 a team of scholars led by Peter Lampe of Heidelberg discovered the site of ancient Pepouza in modern-day Turkey (private communication from Dr. Lampe, November 1, 2001).

6. Hippolytus, *The Refutation of All Heresies* 12, in *Ante-Nicene Fathers* (ed. A. Roberts and J. Donaldson; Peabody, Mass.: Hendrickson, 1994), 5:123.

7. Adolf von Harnack, *History of Dogma* (trans. N. Buchanan; Boston: Little, Brown, 1901), 1:230.

8. Compare in 1 Corinthians the "people of the flesh" (*sarkikoi*, 3:1), the "unspiritual" (*psychikoi*, 2:14), and the "spiritual" (*pneumatikoi*, 2:15).

9. Justin, *Apology* 1.26.

10. Convenient English translations are available in the volume edited by James M. Robinson, *The Nag Hammadi Library in English* (3rd ed.; San Francisco: Harper, 1988).

11. The rejection of Jesus' humanness is known as docetism, from the Greek *dokein*, "to seem [to be]."

12. It is tempting to find a reference to this document in 1 Tim 6:20, "Avoid the profane chatter and contradictions [Greek: *antitheseis*] of what is falsely called

knowledge [Greek: *gnōseōs*]," even though this would require an extremely late date for 1 Timothy. Keep in mind that Marcion did not have 1–2 Timothy or Titus in his collection of Paul's letters.

13. Tertullian, *Against Marcion 2*.

14. Hippolytus, *The Apostolic Tradition* 21.12ff.

15. Translation adapted from John H. Leith, ed., *Creeds of the Churches* (rev. ed.; Richmond, Va.: John Knox Press, 1973), 23.

16. The dispute is therefore known as the Quartodeciman [Fourteenth] Controversy.

17. Tertullian, *Prescription against Heretics* 7:19.

18. Tertullian, *The Flesh of Christ 5*.

19. See David W. Bercat, ed., *A Dictionary of Christian Beliefs* (Peabody, Mass.: Hendrickson, 1998), 272–73.

20. Eusebius, *History* 6.8; most of the information in this paragraph is derived from book 6.

21. Origen, *On First Principles*.

22. Ibid., lviii.

Chapter 3

1. Eusebius, *History* 9.7.

2. On the meaning of the Constantinian reversal for the church and on the concept of "Christendom," see Douglas John Hall, *The Cross in Our Context: Jesus and the Suffering World* (Minneapolis: Fortress Press, 2003), especially chapter 8, "The Theology of the Cross and the Crisis of Christendom."

3. Translation adapted from Michael Grant, *Tacitus: The Annals of Imperial Rome* (Baltimore: Penguin Books, 1971), 365–66.

4. Marcus Aurelius, *Meditations* (trans. G. Long; New York: Chesterfield, n.d.), 11.3.

5. Cited from Will Durant, *Caesar and Christ* (The Story of Civilization: Part 3; New York: Simon & Schuster, 1944), 649.

6. See Roland H. Bainton, *Early Christianity* (Princeton, N.J.: Van Nostrand, 1960), 28–29, 111–17.

7. Jeffery W. Hargis, *Against the Christians: The Rise of Early Anti-Christian Polemic* (New York: Peter Lang, 1999), surveys the anti-Christian writings of Celsus, Porphyry, and the last pagan emperor, Julian (361–363 C.E.).

8. As Hall puts it, "The very idea of a faith whose central image and symbol was a crucified Jew now functioning as the official and (after Theosodius) *only* legal religion of the empire that crucified him—such an idea is absurd and to temporal power unthinkable" (*The Cross in Our Context*, 171–72).

Chapter 4

1. Cited from J. N. D. Kelly, *Early Christian Doctrines* (rev. ed.; New York: Harper & Row, 1978), 339–40.

2. The term "pagan" is used here in a neutral sense as a reference to non-monotheists. It originally denoted country people in distinction from city dwellers.

3. Tertullian, *Against Praxeas 1*, in *Ante-Nicene Fathers* (ed. A. Roberts and J. Donaldson; Peabody, Mass: Hendrickson, 1994), 3:597, adapted.

4. Followers of Nestorius flourished in parts of Syria, Persia, India, and even China (where it was called the "radiant religion of the West"). Nestorians survive to this day in Iraq, parts of Iran, and especially Kurdistan, where they are known as Assyrian Christians and preserve Nestorius's writing, *The Treatise of Heracleides.*

Chapter 5

1. Translation adapted from *The Confessions of St. Augustine* (trans. Edward B. Pusey; New York: Washington Square Press, 1960), 1.

2. See Bercat, *A Dictionary of Christian Beliefs,* 272–73.

3. Manichaeism was a dualistic and syncretistic religion with gnostic overtones founded in Mesopotamia by the prophet Mani in the third century C.E.

4. Neoplatonism was a philosophy founded by Plotinus in the third century that—in contrast to Manichaeism—emphasized the supreme transcendence of the one God and the ultimate goal of mystical oneness of the human being and God.

5. Quoted from the end of book 8 of the *Confessions;* see *The Confessions of St. Augustine,* 147–48.

6. Cf. ibid., 208.

7. Vincent, a monk of Lérins, charged ca. 434 that Augustine's views on grace and predestination were novelties in the church and should be rejected. His formulation of catholicity has become classic: "In the catholic church all possible care should be taken that we hold that faith which has been believed everywhere, always, and by all." Vincent of Lérins, "A Commonitory," 11:132.

Chapter 6

1. Innocent III, *Sicut universitatis conditor,* adapted from Roland H. Bainton, *The Medieval Church* (Princeton, N.J.: Van Nostrand, 1962), 137–38, and from Henry Bettenson, *Documents of the Christian Church* (2nd ed.; London: Oxford University Press, 1963), 155–56.

2. The term "monk" comes from the Greek *monachos,* "living alone," and points to the original form of monasticism, the life of the hermit. The word "hermit" comes from the Greek *ērēmos,* "desert." "Nun" is from the Latin *nonna,* "chaste," "holy."

3. Philip Schaff, *History of the Christian Church* (5th ed.; Grand Rapids, Mich.: Eerdmans, 1981), 3:155.

4. Alfred Tennyson memorialized Simeon in the poem, "Simeon Stylites," cited from Schaff, *History of the Christian Church,* 3:193–94:

> Although I be the basest of mankind,
> From scalp to sole one slough and crust of sin,
> Unfit for earth, unfit for heaven, scarce meet
> For troops of devils, mad with blasphemy,
> I will not cease to grasp the hope I hold
> Of saintdom, and to clamor, moan, and sob,
> Battering the gates of heaven with storms of prayer:
> Have mercy, Lord, and take away my sin.
>
> . . .
>
> Thou knowest I bore this better at the first,

For I was strong and hale of body then;
And though my teeth, which now are dropt away,
Would chatter with the cold, and all my beard
Was tagged with icy fringes in the moon,
I drowned the whoopings of the owl with sound
Of pious hymns and psalms, and sometimes saw
An angel stand and watch me, as I sang.
Now I am feeble grown: my end draws nigh—
I hope my end draws nigh: half dead am I,
So that I scarce can hear the people hum
About the column's base; and almost blind,
And scarce can recognize the fields I know.
And both my thighs are rotted with the dew,
Yet cease I not to clamor and to cry,
While my stiff spine can hold my weary head,
Till all my limbs drop piecemeal from the stone.
Have mercy, mercy; take away my sin.

5. Eusebius, *History* 6.43.11. See also Peter Lampe, *From Paul to Valentinus: Christians at Rome in the First Two Centuries* (trans. M. Steinhauser; ed. M. Johnson; Minneapolis: Fortress Press, 2003), 143.

6. A noteworthy exception is an Egyptian monk, Paphnutius (d. ca. 360), a disciple of Antony who suffered severely during the last persecution. At the Council of Nicea he dissuaded the bishops from ordering all clergy to put away their wives, arguing that sexual intercourse in marriage was honorable and spotless. See Schaff, *History of the Christian Church,* 3:244–45.

7. Cyprian, Epistle 62.13, in *Ante-Nicene Fathers* (ed. A. Roberts and J. Donaldson; Peabody, Mass: Hendrickson, 1994), 5:384–85.

8. Cyprian, *On the Unity of the Catholic Church* 6, in *Ante-Nicene Fathers* 5: 423.

9. Cyprian, Epistle 66.7, in *Ante-Nicene Fathers* 3:375.

10. See William J. La Due, *The Chair of Saint Peter: A History of the Papacy* (Maryknoll, N.Y.: Orbis, 1999).

11. Leo I gained enormous prestige by twice saving Rome from destruction—by Attila the Hun in 452 and by the Vandals in 455.

12. The tradition emerged that the apostle Andrew had founded the church at Constantinople, and Byzantine theologians observed that Jesus in the New Testament called Andrew before calling his brother, Peter—founder of the church at Rome.

13. Justinian deported Pope Vigilius and later Pope Martin to Constantinople, where they were forced to acknowledge themselves as humble servants of the emperor.

14. Adapted from John of Damascus, *On the Divine Images* (trans. David Anderson; Crestwood, N.Y.: St. Vladimir's Seminary Press, 1980), 23–24.

15. Cited from Will Durant, *The Age of Faith* (vol. 4 of *The Story of Civilization*; New York: Simon & Schuster, 1950), 544.

16. Fearful of dissidence, this council also condemned John Huss to death. He was burned at the stake in July 1415.

Chapter 7

1. Published from manuscript by George B. Flahiff, "Deus Non Vult: A Critic of the Third Crusade," *Medieval Studies* 9 (1947): 162–88, cited by Bainton, *The Medieval Church*, 119–20.

2. Several English translations are available; used here is the translation by N. J. Dawood, *The Koran* (Baltimore: Penguin Books, 1974).

3. A classic work on the crusades is Steven Runciman, *A History of the Crusades* (3 vols; Cambridge: Cambridge University Press, 1952–54). See also Jonathan Riles Jones, ed., *The Oxford Illustrated History of the Crusades* (Oxford: Oxford University Press, 1995).

4. A conflation of sources translated by Dana Carlton Monroe, "Urban and the Crusaders," in *Translations and Reprints* (Philadelphia: University of Pennsylvania, 1901); cited by Bainton, *The Medieval Church*, 118.

5. Estimates of the numbers of persons involved in any of the crusades vary widely; see Runciman, "The Numerical Strength of the Crusaders," Appendix 2 in *A History of the Crusades*, 1:336–41.

6. Raymond of Agiles, *Historia Francorum* (trans. F. Duncalf and A. C. Krey; New York: Harper, 1912); cited in Bainton, *The Medieval Church*, 119.

Chapter 8

1. This wording is adapted from a wall hanging I purchased at a gift shop in Assisi, Italy. The prayer is available in various forms on websites and in print. For example, see Leonardo Boff, *The Prayer of Saint Francis* (trans. Phillip Berryman; Maryknoll, N.Y.: Orbis, 2001), 95–98.

2. Abélard (d. 1142) in his famous *Sic et Non* (Yes and No) arranged extracts of the church fathers on each doctrine without providing a synthesis or a resolution— so that they seemed to contradict each other.

3. Anselm's title for the treatise in which he makes this argument is *Cur deus homo?* (Why the God-man?).

4. Peter Abélard, *The Story of My Misfortunes* (trans. H. A. Bellows; New York: Macmillan, 1922).

5. The five arguments are found also in *Summa Theologica* I, question 2, article 3.

6. Aristotle distinguished four kinds of causation: (1) formal, which is the pattern or conception of something that can come into being; (2) material, which is the matter or substance from which the thing will come into being; (3) efficient, the actions that are required for the thing to come into being; and (4) final, which is the functioning or raison d'être of the thing.

7. The term "dunce" comes from later humanists who ridiculed scholasticism.

8. Gabriel Biel, an Occamist at Tübingen, was a teacher of John Nathin, one of Luther's teachers at Erfurt.

9. Cf. Margaret Deanesly, *A History of the Medieval Church, 590–1500* (8th ed.; London: Methuen, 1954), 234.

10. These are included in Hildegard of Bingen, *Scivias* (trans. Columba Hart and Jane Bishop; New York: Paulist Press, 1990). A concise introduction to Hildegard's life and work is provided by Rosemary Radford Ruether, *Visionary Women: Three Medieval Mystics* (Minneapolis: Fortress Press, 2002), 6–29.

11. See *Hildegard of Bingen's Book of Divine Works with Letters and Songs* (ed. Matthew Fox; Santa Fe, N.M.: Bear & Co., 1987).

12. Thomas à Kempis, *The Imitation of Christ* (trans. Leo Sherley-Price; Middlesex, England: Penguin Books, 1952), book 2, chap. 3, pp. 70–71.

Chapter 9

1. Adapted from the translation by Bertram Lee Woolf, *Reformation Writings of Martin Luther* (New York: Philosophical Library, 1956), 289. A translation by Charles M. Jacobs can be found in *Luther's Works* (ed. J. Pelikan and H. Lehman; Philadelphia: Fortress Press, 1960), 35:370–71.

2. For example, Sebastian Brant's poem, "Narrenschyff" (Ship of fools); cited by Bainton, *The Medieval Church,* 186:

> St. Peter's bark now lists and pitches.
> I fear she will be food for fishes.
>
> . . .
>
> Seldom is the truth now heard,
> For men pervert God's Holy Word.
>
> . . .
>
> Seeing the like I'm bound to say
> We're not far off the judgment day.

3. In 1524 Erasmus published *De libero arbitrio* (On the freedom of the will), to which Luther responded in 1525 with what he considered his greatest work, *De servo arbitrio* (On the bondage of the will).

4. Anne in Christian tradition is the mother of the Virgin Mary.

5. The sacrament of penance in Roman Catholic theology is based on the idea that, although God alone can impose and remove eternal punishment for sin, the church imposes on the sinner temporal punishment that can be worked off in this life and in purgatory by acts of penance, devotion, or good works. An indulgence is a remission of all (plenary) or part of this temporal punishment. The Jubilee Indulgence was inaugurated by Pope Julius II (1503–1513) to finance the rebuilding of St. Peter's and, after much hesitation, renewed by Pope Leo X. It was now determined that when indulgences were purchased by proxy for departed souls in purgatory, contrition and confession would not be required of the purchaser. Tetzel is reputed to have marketed indulgences with such jingles as: "As soon as the coin in the coffer rings, the soul from purgatory springs."

6. No council would meet until 1545, at which time the Council of Trent solidified anti-Protestant doctrines and discipline.

7. Adapted from Roland Bainton, *Here I Stand: A Life of Martin Luther* (Nashville: Abingdon Press, 1950), 185. A minority of scholars consider some or all of these words to be apocryphal.

8. How the Constitution of the United States came to say what it does about freedom of religion is summarized by Frank Lambert, *The Founding Fathers and the Place of Religion in America* (Princeton, N.J.: Princeton University Press, 2003). Lambert quotes Thomas Jefferson: "Almighty God has created the mind free and manifested his supreme will that free it shall remain by making it altogether unsusceptible of restraint; that all attempts to influence it by temporal punishments, or burthens, or by civil incapacitations, tend only to beget habits of hypocrisy and

meanness, and are a departure from the plan of the holy author of our religion" (233–34). See also chapter 10, "Rationalism."

9. In 1524 Luther wrote against the radicals, whom he sometimes called "Schwärmer" (visionary religious fanatics), in his treatise "Against the Heavenly Prophets," in *Luther's Works* (Philadelphia: Fortress Press, 1958), 40:73–223.

10. *On Jews and Their Lies* (trans. Martin H. Bertram), in *Luther's Works* (Philadelphia: Fortress Press, 1971), 47:121–306.

11. "I ask that no one make reference to my name. Let them call themselves Christians, not Lutherans. What is Luther? After all, the teaching is not mine. Neither was I crucified for anyone" (*Luther's Works* [Philadelphia: Fortress Press, 1962], 45:71).

12. Zwingli asserted that the words "this is my body . . . my blood" in the words of institution refer only to the divine nature of Christ, not the human, and that *finitum non capax infiniti*, "the finite is not capable of the infinite." Luther by contrast emphasized the unity of Christ, that the finite is indeed capable of conveying the infinite, and that if Jesus said "this is" that is exactly what he meant. (The Semitic languages Hebrew and Aramaic, however, have no common copulative verb.)

13. The original title of the Latin document is *Christianae Religionis Institutio*.

14. Servetus, who was physician to the archbishop of Vienne from 1541 to 1553, is credited with the discovery of the circulation of the blood and also with a method for canning vegetables and fruits. See Roland H. Bainton, *Hunted Heretic: The Life and Death of Michael Servetus 1511–1553* (Boston: Beacon Press, 1953).

15. See Brian Moynahan, *God's Bestseller: William Tyndale, Thomas More, and the Writing of the English Bible—A Story of Martyrdom and Betrayal* (New York: St. Martin's Press, 2002).

16. Ibid., 1.

17. Luther A. Weigle, "English Versions of the Bible," in *The New Oxford Annotated Bible with the Apocrypha* (ed. Herbert G. May and Bruce M. Metzger; New York and Oxford: Oxford University Press, 1977), 1552.

18 Ibid., 1553.

Chapter 10

1. Philip Jacob Spener, *Pia Desideria* (trans. and ed. T. G. Tappert; Philadelphia: Fortress Press, 1964), 36–37.

2. James H. Nichols, *History of Christianity* 1650–1950 (New York: The Ronald Press, 1956), 42.

3. The *Book of Concord* contains the three ancient creeds (Apostles', Nicene, Athanasian), the "Augsburg Confession," the "Apology of the Augsburg Confession," the "Smalcald Articles," Luther's "Small Catechism," Luther's "Large Catechism," "Treatise on the Power and Primacy of the Pope," and the "Formula of Concord." The most recent English translation is edited by Robert Kolb and Timothy J. Wengert (Minneapolis: Fortress Press, 2000). See also Günther Gassmann and Scott Hendrix, *Fortress Introduction to the Lutheran Confessions* (Minneapolis: Fortress Press, 1999).

4. The concepts of the "plenary inspiration" and "verbal inerrancy" of the Bible appear to have emerged during doctrinal disputes between Lutheran and Calvinist orthodoxists.

5. *The Theologia Germanica of Martin Luther* (trans. Bengt Hoffman; New York: Paulist, 1980).

6. Spener, *Pia Desideria.*

7. A certain Neumeister, a hymnologist of Hamburg, closed his Ascension Day sermon in 1722 by distributing the hymn:

> "Go out into the world," the Lord of old did say;
> But now, "Where God has placed thee,
> *There* he would have thee stay!"

See A. L. Drummond, *German Protestantism since Luther* (London: Epworth, 1951), 62.

See also Timothy George, *Faithful Witness* (Birmingham: New Hope, 1991), 39.

8. Some of his hymns, like "Jesus, Thy Blood and Righteousness," are still used today.

9. Cited by W. Walker et al., *A History of the Christian Church* (4th ed.; New York: Scribner's, 1985), 601.

10. In 1724 Anthony Collins published some pamphlets that demolished the argument from prophecy by showing that these were mostly cases of prophecy after the event. In 1748, in his "Essay on Miracles," David Hume showed the fallacy of the argument from miracles; miracles could never be proved sufficiently to build a religion on them and even if they did happen we could never prove that the cause of the suspension of natural law was God. The arguments from prophecy and from miracles are nonetheless still heard today.

11. Immanuel Kant, *Religion within the Limits of Reason Alone* (trans. T. Greene and H. Hudson; New York: Harper, 1960). His major philosophical writings are *Critique of Pure Reason* (1781) and *Critique of Practical Reason* (1788). Kant's earliest writings were in science; his philosophical and religious works were written when he was fifty-seven to sixty-nine years old.

12. Kant, *Religion within the Limits,* 101, note.

13. Athanasius was the most zealous defender of the doctrine of the Trinity in the fourth century; see chapter 4.

14. Albert E. Bergh, ed., *The Writings of Thomas Jefferson* (20 vols.; Washington, D.C., 1903–1904), 15:383–85.

15. Nichols, *History of Christianity,* 50–51.

16. Hermann Samuel Reimarus, *Fragments* (Philadelphia: Fortress Press, 1970). See also Albert Schweitzer, *The Quest of the Historical Jesus* (New York: Macmillan, 1968), chapter 2.

17. Adapted from the translation by Kenneth W. Appelgate, *Voltaire on Religion* (New York: Frederick Unger, 1974), 212–13.

18. William Law, *A Serious Call to a Devout and Holy Life* (1728); George Berkeley, *Alciphron* (1732); Joseph Butler, *Analogy of Religion* (1736).

19. Allegory treats narratives as continuous metaphor, in which the interpreter takes each detail to correspond to a "spiritual" or theological meaning. Typology is a more restricted Christian comparison of Old Testament details to aspects of the ministry, death, or resurrection of Jesus. Both methods leave the interpreter more or less free to ignore the context out of which the text originated.

20. Although allegorical interpretation was the preferred method of interpretation among early Christian scholars at Alexandria (Clement and Origen, for

example), some scholars at Antioch, notably Theodore of Mopsuestia (ca. 350–428), attempted to discern the original setting of a text. And, in spite of his christological reading of Old Testament texts, Martin Luther was able to draw on historical arguments regarding the non-apostolic authorship of some New Testament books, for example, James and Jude. See his "Preface to the Epistles of St. James and St. Jude," in *Luther's Works,* 35:395-98.

21. Surveys of the history of the interpretation of the New Testament (but with considerable information on the Old Testament as well) are given by William Baird, *History of New Testament Research* (2 vols.; Minneapolis: Fortress Press, 1992, 2002), and by Werner George Kümmel, *The New Testament: The History of the Investigation of Its Problems* (trans. S. M. Gilmour and H. C. Kee; Nashville: Abindon, 1972). Kümmel includes extended quotations from the scholars surveyed. The older survey, "History of the Interpretation of the Bible," by Robert M. Grant, John T. McNeill, and Samuel Terrien, in *The Interpreter's Bible* (12 vols.; Nashville: Abingdon, 1952), 1:106-141, is still valuable.

22. Baird, *History of New Testament Research,* 1:17.

23. Semler refers to Jesus' words in Mark 4:33, "He spoke the word to them, *as they were able to hear it."*

24. Friedrich D. E. Schleiermacher (1768–1834) sought to overcome the impasse among the post-Reformation movements by beginning with the category of feeling and moving from there to a full-blown systematic theology that would describe the beliefs and ideals of the Christian church in a compelling way to a jaded public. His accomplishment has earned him the epithet "founder of modern (or liberal) theology." In his classic work, *The Christian Faith* (1821–1822), (trans. H. R. Mackintosh and J. S. Stewart [New York: Harper, 1963]), he used the expression "immediate self-consciousness" to clarify what he meant by feeling. Religion, Schleiermacher suggested, is the "feeling of absolute dependence." Reflection on this feeling leads to awareness of self, the world, and God. An individual's relationship to the world is one of reciprocity, not absolute dependence. God can be defined as that to which we feel absolutely dependent. Our relationship to God is characterized by freedom with respect to thought but dependence with respect to doing.

Chapter 11

1. It seems that Galileo quoted his contemporary Baronius; see, for example, Philip J. Sampson, *6 Modern Myths about Christianity and Western Civilization* (Downers Grove, Ill.: InterVarsity, 2001), chapter 1.

2. In Charles Hodge, *What Is Darwinism?* (New York: Scribner's, Armstrong, and Company, 1874).

3. Hans Schwarz, *Evil: A Historical and Theological Perspective* (trans. Mark W. Worthing; Lima, Ohio: Academic Renewal Press, 2001), 18.

4. Freud's *Moses and Monotheism* (New York: Knopf, 1949) is a fascinating interpretation of the origin of Israelite religion. Richard L. Rubenstein in *My Brother Paul* (New York: Harper, 1972) applied a Freudian interpretation to central Christian doctrines in Paul's letters.

5. See Harding Meyer, *That All May Be One: Perceptions and Models of Ecumenicity* (trans. William G. Rusch; Grand Rapids, Mich.: Eerdmans, 1999).

6. The following sketch is largely dependent on Robert McAfee Brown, "Ecumenical Movement," *The Encyclopedia of Religion,* ed. Mircea Eliade (New York: Macmillan, 1987), 5:17–27.

7. Gillian R. Evans, *Method in Ecumenical Theology: The Lessons So Far* (Cambridge: Cambridge University Press, 1996), 1.

Chapter 12

1. Søren Kierkegaard, *Attack upon Christendom* (trans. Walter Lowrie; Boston: Beacon, 1944), 33.

2. Dietrich Bonhoeffer, *Letters and Papers from Prison* (London: SCM Press, 1953), 91.

3. On postmodernity and Christian theology in general, see Paul Lakeland, *Postmodernity: Christian Identity in a Fragmented Age* (Guides to Theological Inquiry; Minneapolis: Fortress Press, 1997). Helpful also to understand the concept are Gianni Vattimo, *The End of Modernity: Nihilism and Hermeneutics in Postmodern Culture* (trans. Jon R. Snyder; Baltimore: Johns Hopkins University Press, 1988) and Alister E. McGrath, *Reality* (vol. 2 of A Scientific Theology; Grand Rapids, Mich.: Eerdmans, 2002).

4. For some of the following comments I am indebted to the summary of James C. Livingston, *Modern Christian Thought* (rev. ed., 2 vols.; New York: Macmillan, 1997, 2000), 1:385–97.

5. Søren Kierkegaard, *Philosophical Fragments* (Princeton, N.J.: Princeton University Press, 1952), 87.

6. James C. Livingston, *Modern Christian Thought* (orig. ed.; New York: Macmillan, 1971), 323f.

7. The following comments on Nietzsche are based in part on Livingston's summary in *Modern Christian Thought* (rev. ed.), 1:397–412.

8. The parable of the Madman is in *The Gay Science*; cited by Livingston, *Modern Christian Thought* (rev. ed.), 1:400.

9. Typical of such an approach is the still readable *What Is Christianity?* by Adolph Harnack (trans. T. B. Saunders; Philadelphia: Fortress Press, 1957). Albrecht Ritschl (1822–1889) is another paradigm of this approach.

10. Barth's magnum opus is his many-volumed *Church Dogmatics* (Edinburgh: T&T Clark, 1936–1969).

11. Examples of pioneering works on feminist theology are Patricia Wilson-Kastner, *Faith, Feminism, and the Christ* (Philadelphia: Fortress Press, 1983); Susan Brooks Thistlethwaite, *Sex, Race, and God: Christian Feminism in Black and White* (New York: Crossroad, 1989); and Rosemary Radford Ruether, *Sexism and God-Talk: Toward a Feminist Theology* (Boston: Beacon, 1983).

12. Such are the views of one of the pioneers of liberation theology, Gustavo Gutiérrez, in *A Theology of Liberation* (trans. and ed. C. Inda and J. Eagleson; Maryknoll, N.Y.: Orbis, 1973).

13. On postmodern biblical interpretation in general, see A. K. M. Adam, *Handbook of Postmodern Biblical Interpretation* (St. Louis: Chalice Press, 2000). Brueggemann's program for biblical interpretation in a postmodern context is laid out in his *Texts under Negotiation: The Bible and Postmodern Imagination* (Minneapolis: Fortress Press, 1993), although it is anticipated in such books as *The*

Prophetic Imagination (2nd ed.; Minneapolis: Fortress Press, 2001; orig. ed., 1978) and *The Message of the Psalms* (Minneapolis: Augsburg, 1984) and undergirds his magisterial *Theology of the Old Testament* (Minneapolis: Fortress Press, 1997).

14. Douglas John Hall, *Lighten Our Darkness: Towards an Indigenous Theology of the Cross* (rev. ed.; Lima, Ohio: Academic Renewal Press, 2001).

15. See, for example, Douglas John Hall, *Thinking the Faith: Christian Theology in a North American Context* (Minneapolis: Augsburg, 1989), especially 200–7.

16. Hall, *The Cross in Our Context,* especially chapter 8, "The Theology of the Cross and the Crisis of Christendom."

17. John Milbank, *The Word Made Strange: Theology, Language, Culture* (Oxford, U.K., and Cambridge, Mass.: Blackwell, 1997); Milbank, *Theology and Social Theory* (Oxford, U.K., and Cambridge, Mass.: Blackwell, 1990); Milbank, with Catherine Pickstock and Graham Ward, eds., *Radical Orthodoxy: A New Theology* (London and New York: Routledge, 1999).

18. Milbank et al., *Radical Orthodoxy,* 1.

19. Milbank, *Theology and Social Theory,* 2.

20. Milbank et al., *Radical Orthodoxy,* 2.

Epilogue

1. Roy A. Harrisville and Walter Sundberg, *The Bible in Modern Culture* (2nd ed.; Grand Rapids, Mich.: Eerdmans, 2002), 86–87.

2. See J. N. D. Kelly, *Early Christian Creeds* (3rd ed.; New York: McKay, 1972), 76–88, and, for example, Thomas F. Torrance, *The Trinitarian Faith* (Edinburgh: T&T Clark, 1988), 34–39 et passim.

3. For a reconstruction of the emergence of "normative Christianity," see Hultgren, *The Rise of Normative Christianity.*

Index